2016: THE GANG'S ALL HERE!

Welcome to the Second Captains Sports Annual, Volume 2!

We are monumentally pumped to bring you this record of the year that was – a rollocking, roller-coaster 12 months which saw Robbie Brady and his weeping brother sweep into our lives; Ryan Lochte create an international incident; Pat Hickey become one of the stars of the Rio Olympics; and Ronaldo get attacked by a giant moth in front of a global audience.

Let's be honest though, 2016 was grim. We lost Bowie, we lost Prince and there's only so much the introduction of the O'Donovan brothers can make up for. But we at least have some wondrous moments at Euro 2016 to look back on; the three unforgettable Irish goals, redemption in 30 seconds for Wes against Italy, Hendrick antagonising France on the deck when we were 0-1 up! What memories. Yes, Muhammad Ali may no longer be with us but we will always have that Daryl Murphy backheel.

It was the year of the f-bomb – from Michael Conlan, to Danny Baker's tweets, to a man named Bubbles, unrestrained exclamations of joy and despair defined our sporting year.

In these very pages, Eoin talks to our world champion amateur boxer about his Olympic nightmare, Ken meets Richard Dunne, and then takes us on a very personal journey through the Euros, while there's Kabaddi advice from Oisin McConville, Annalise Murphy-inspired sailing tips with four-time Rush Regatta winner Simon Hick, and a word from our wonderful Icelandic ambassador Anton Ingi Sveinbjörnsson. Some of your favourite features from last year's book such as The Marseille Years and the amazing illustrations of CIEMAY also make a welcome return.

As 2016 prepares to meet its maker, we offer this pithy, 112-page obituary (only it's one of those hilarious obituaries, with gags and cartoons and things). We hope it again brings back some warm annual memories from years gone by.

ENJOY.

Second Captains
xx

FEATURING

INTRODUCING OUR NEW MASCOT!

Let us introduce you to the newest member of the Second Captains team, it's Stephen the Second Captains Stink Badger! Don't be fooled by the unfortunate name, the stink badger is not typically a smelly animal. Not in Stephen's case however, he IS a smelly bastard. We're not talking about foul-smelling secretions that stink badgers sometimes expel from their anal glands in self-defence, he just smells of cigarettes. Plus he never really washes his sweatshirt. Stephen will guide you through certain sections of the annual, and we won't lie, he has no sporting or journalistic ability. But he's black and white and so is our logo so we didn't over-think it.

Factfile

Stephen the Second Captains Stink Badger Factfile:

- Stephen wears his favourite green sweatshirt and red shirt at all-times in honour of his hero Brian Clough.
- He still talks ill of the late Don Revie but does acknowledge him as being a great "football man".
- He vapes as he is addicted to nicotine
- He wears no pants like Goleo (see right) and he feels no embarrassment in shirt-cocking whilst still wearing dress shoes.
- He will not be fooled by twig-snapping sound.
- He sometimes gets drunk on rotten apples.
- He loves the speedway coverage on Sky Sports.
- He is not a journalist, he found the hat on the barstool of a Navan pub after it was left behind by a stag party and uses it now as a conversation starter.

STEPHEN THE STINK BADGER

OUR SHITE MASCOTS TOP 3

1. Kingsley of Partick Thistle

The most terrifying mascot known to humanity, Kingsley was designed by the Turner Prize-winning artist David Shrigley in 2015. The mascot caused a global stir when it was unveiled and aside from making all the kids who go to Partick Thistle games cry, Kingsley has been known to intimidate opponents with its pitch-side angry death stare. Even our shitty mascot Stephen has better looks.

2 - Murty of Munster

Clearly the shittiest mascot the sporting world has ever produced, Murty was correctly sent to his death bed and a plastic recycling plant in 2012. Was it because of the flagrant breach of former Ireland prop Tony Buckley's image rights or because it was so shite? We'll never know.

3 - Goleo

We've no real problem with this giant lion who was the mascot for the 2006 FIFA World Cup in Germany – even though he received real criticism for not being a German animal, but rather the emblem of historical rivals England and the Netherlands. He makes this list simply because he wore no trousers or underwear (shirt-cocked) wherever he went, even to high class events with Pele.

HONOURABLE MENTION:
Dr Dunk of the National Basketball Arena

Doctor Dunk was prescribing good vibes around the Tallaght arena in the 90s. However our sources tell us that the doctor himself may have occasionally required treatment, having been constantly struck down by beatings from bored local teenagers and kids who found assaulting a giant basketball far more entertaining than the basketball itself. The doctor was a giant round basketball and despite an extensive nationwide search, no photos remain of this legend of the mascot world – that's how shite he was.

I ♥ MY DOGS

At home with:

RICHIE SADLIER

RICHIE SADLIER IS A MUCH-BELOVED FACE ON IRISH TELEVISION, RECOGNISED ACROSS THE COUNTRY FOR HIS BALD HEAD, SMOOTH-TALKING WAYS, SEXUAL CHARISMA, AND HIS PENCHANT FOR DISAGREEING WITH OLDER MEN ON LIVE TV. BUT AWAY FROM THE TV SCREEN, RICHIE IS A RECLUSE, LIVING IN THE WOODS AND PREFERRING TO FOCUS ALL OF HIS ATTENTION ON HIS TWO GREAT LOVES - DOGS AND CARPENTRY. HERE, FOR THE FIRST TIME, WE GET TO CLIMB INSIDE HIS TREEHOUSE HOME. WELCOME TO THE WEIRD AND WONDERFUL WORLD OF RICHIE SADLIER!

1.

It's been 12 days since Richie last left the house, but who cares about that when you've got dogs a-plenty? Truly dogs are a man's best friend – they're loyal, they're obedient, they don't disagree with you on whether Dundalk's success is good for the league in general – sorry Peter Collins, but these guys are Richie's BFFs. Fun Fact: Off camera, Richie only wears dog-themed clothing. Cool t-shirt Richie!

RICHIE'S SCOOBY SNACKS!

2.

When ensconced in his woodland retreat, far from the madding crowd, Richie and his beloved new dog Bobbi like nothing better than play-time in the kitchen. Here they are preparing over-sized biscuits for dinner. Sure, the 'h' spelt out in dog-friendly fake chocolate sauce is a little wonky, but Bobbi doesn't have opposable thumbs, cut the girl some slack. Wow, they came out perfectly!! Richie looks delighted, Bobbi a little less so. She seems to woof – "why does everything he eat have to be in the shape of a bone? Isn't that a little… strange?" Shut up and eat your biscuit Bobbi!!

3.

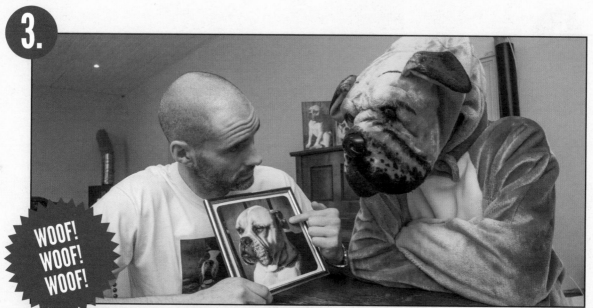

WOOF! WOOF! WOOF!

Some people trying to figure out why Richie has retreated so completely from public life have sought to attach some importance to the tragic death of his first dog, Frank. But of course, that's ridiculous. Sure, Richie's hired a trained psychologist to live with him 24/7 and walk around dressed as Frank in an attempt to get over his death, but wouldn't we all do that, given the chance? Here he is talking through some issues with Declan, who Richie insists on calling… Frank. You're such a good listener Declan, I mean Frank!

4.

It's not ALL about dogs and carpentry of course. Here's Richie's glittering trophy cabinet, which serves as a reminder of his glorious time at the top. What a competitive year that was at Broadford Rovers! So many memories!!!

5.

Back in the old days, Richie was a swinging blade on the Dublin social scene. Today he's much happier engaging in simpler, nobler passions. Sorry Duffer, this man's phone is off… because what could possibly be better than an evening in watching your favourite movie, 'Marley and Me'? Or sitting outside with your favourite book? When there's so much to learn, human interaction can only serve as a distraction from your important work – making dogs out of wood! He just loves dogs! And carpentry of course!

6.

Richie once tried to tell Ronnie Whelan about the therapeutic effects of a bit of carpentry, but he was having none of it. So Richie is happy to indulge his love of carpentry in splendid isolation. He crafted his own treehouse home with his bare hands. Sure, it doesn't have plumbing in any real sense, but he and his dogs are happy roaming the woods nearby, defecating where they please.

7.

Here are a few of his most prized carpentry successes –

- a wagon for when he and the dogs want to go on road-trips. He often invites Declan and his binman Glen along for the ride too – after they've dressed up as dogs first of course!

- and his life's work – no not arguing with Liam and Eamon! - this is The Marauding Richie, the boat he's been working on for the past 15 years. Here he is adding the finishing touches! Once complete, Richie plans to finally leave his home in the woods and sail down the liffey with over 1500 dogs on board. There might even be room for Glen and Declan! All aboard the Marauding Richie!

THE EUROS DIARY

Ken Early on a summer of football, hooligans, and Brexit

From a riot on opening night, through to an anti-climactic defeat in the final for a host country just happy to get through the tournament without incident, the month gave us a stark picture of a Europe growing increasingly divided.

It was the month of Robbie Brady and Bale and Brexit, of Go-Pros and No Surrender. Ireland, England, Wales and Northern Ireland all contributed on the field, but was this the summer when the European football family failed to distract us from the continental storm threatening to envelop us?

U.K. RETAIL SALES VOLUME
MONTH-OVER-MONTH CHANGE
2.0%
1.5
1.0
1.9%

U.K. PMI OUTPUT INDEXES
60
55 MANUFACTURING
50
55 SERVICES
50
45
BREXIT VOTE
CONSTRUCTION
JAN. 2016   AUG. 2016

CHANGE IN U.K. STOCK MARKET
15%
FTSE 100 INDEX
10
5
S&P 5
0
DAY FOLLOWING BREXIT VOTE
-5
JUNE 2016   SEPT. 2016
SOURCES: BLOOMBERG, MARKIT, S&P GLOBAL

SCATTERING PLANE
PRINCIPAL
AZIMUTH PLANE

1A

WE'RE OUT!

After 43 years' UK freed from shackles of EU

PM in crisis as voters reject Project Fear

Leave surge sends pound to a 31-year low

SUR LE PONT D'AVIGNON, AND SONGS AT O'MALLEYS

It's a sunny Wednesday evening in June, and I'm sitting at a cafe table in Marseille's Place de Lenche, looking down past the Old Port to the spire of Basilique Notre Dame de la Garde.

Euro 2016 kicks off in two days' time. Once the tournament starts there won't be much time to enjoy just being in France, so I came a couple of days early to acclimatise.

I spent the morning getting sunburnt walking down the coast road, and the afternoon up in Avignon visiting the palace of the anti-Pope. Avignon has a famous bridge to nowhere that juts out into the middle of the Rhone and stops in mid-stream. You wonder how they could possibly have built a massive stone bridge like this in the 14th century. They must have thought it would last forever, but most of it was swept away in a flood 350 years ago.

Now I'm back in this sun-dappled square eating seared tuna steak and drinking white wine. My life has turned into a Sunday evening ITV travel show.

48 hours later civilisation in Marseille hasn't quite collapsed, but you could say it is buffering. Flying bottles, tear gas, ranks of French riot cops, and confused people standing around trying to figure out what is going on.

> AS THE NIGHT GOES ON I FEEL SAFER NEAR THE CROWDS OF ENGLAND FANS THAN WANDERING THE STREETS ALONE. ADMITTEDLY THAT'S MAINLY BECAUSE I'M WORRIED ABOUT BEING MISTAKEN FOR AN ENGLAND FAN.

Who started it? The English are blaming local hoods who come running out of the back streets to launch unprovoked attacks on the peace-loving English fans. Everyone else is blaming the English. It must be them, there was no trouble before they got here.

To the English, this seems unfair. All they've done is drink and sing. Sure, they have been drinking and singing in a way that can come across as rather boorish and could even be seen as laying down a challenge to the local tough guys. But there's nothing illegal about that, is there?

When the bar where I'm watching France play Romania in the opening game is suddenly attacked by a bunch of locals who come running down a back street to throw bottles and overturn tables, I realise there is some truth to what the England fans are saying. As the night goes on I feel safer near the crowds of England fans than wandering the streets alone. Admittedly that's mainly because I'm worried about being mistaken for an England fan.

For all the fear and confusion, there is something comical about that Friday night. Like O'Malley's, the Irish pub that cheerfully danced with the devil, serving booze to the crowd all day and all night and ending up having to close when a policeman inadvertently shot a tear gas canister inside and cleared out the bar.

GO-PROS, TRIBUTE ACTS AND BILLY RAY CYRUS

(SATURDAY, JUNE 11)

On the Saturday afternoon the Russians come, and things aren't funny any more. There are about 150 serious hooligans who know how to fight and they have come specifically to hunt down and destroy their English equivalents.

But there are no English equivalents. The English used to have hooligans like this but they've been weeded out by banning orders and old age. Today's England fans are a tribute act. Even the aggressive, confrontational ones are more interested in macho posturing than actual violence.

The chants have lost their old edge. You will still hear the occasional *No Surrender* or *Fuck off ISIS* but the main song is *Don't Take Me Home*, sung to the tune of Billy Ray Cyrus' *Achy Breaky Heart*. It's a mournful dirge on the theme of mitching off work.

The Russians are more like a paramilitary unit. Their field equipment includes MMA gloves and GoPros to record the ultraviolence. Not for Putin the self-defeating English policy of banning likely trouble-makers from travel. Robbed of their best men, the English are no match for these psychopaths. All day Saturday the English are terrorised. You can imagine the old boys at home, snarling at TV images of the rout.

The English pain is compounded by injustice. No Russian hooligan wears team colours but almost all England fans do, which makes them a lot easier to identify. Lacking an accurate picture of what is going on and struggling to think of a better idea, the riot police settle for lobbing tear gas at the frightened English crowd.

The English have been abandoned even by their own media, which treacherously labels them a national disgrace. Their attitude disgusts the fans. Typical dishonesty from the MSM. One day it'll be payback time…

> **THE ENGLISH USED TO HAVE HOOLIGANS LIKE THIS BUT THEY'VE BEEN WEEDED OUT BY BANNING ORDERS AND OLD AGE. TODAY'S ENGLAND FANS ARE A TRIBUTE ACT.**

***

The Velodrome has recently been revamped with the addition of a curved white shell-like roof. It looks good from outside but from the inside it looks a bit flimsy and paper-like. These big stands should be open to the sky.

Down on the pitch England perform with ponderous, methodical competence and take the lead in the second half when Eric Dier hammers in a free-kick. But the very last Russian break ends with a deep cross and a looping header by their ancient captain, Berezutskiy, that floats over the head of Joe Hart and in.

As the whistle goes, something strange starts to happen in the stand behind Hart's goal. You can see a mass movement from left to right, as people advance from the Russian side of the stand and retreat from the English side. At the edge of the stand, England fans are pouring over a barrier in obvious panic. Russians are running up the stand and seizing England flags that have been abandoned by their fleeing owners. Later they will proudly display the captured trophies on social media.

It's after midnight and getting back to my apartment is complicated. The metro has apparently closed. There are rumours that an English fan has been pushed onto the train tracks and killed. The story turns out to have been fabricated by the troll news network, *Forest Echo News*, but it spreads quickly enough that even the French volunteers in the media centre are repeating it. There is no way to tell whether there's still violence going on outside. This is one of those nights when malicious disinformation just doesn't seem that funny.

11.06.16

GRIMBERGEN, KISS-CAMS AND THE KINGS OF CRAIC

(SUNDAY, MONDAY JUNE 12/13)

The next morning I sleep all the way up to Paris on the train and go to the Parc des Princes for Turkey-Croatia. Luka Modric scores the winner in the first half with a freakish dipping volley from 30 yards.

Afterwards a few of us get food in a place near the stadium that is showing Germany v Ukraine. It's a bad game and the only beer they have on draught is Grimbergen. After a couple of Grimbergens I realise I've already started to shout and slur my words. It turns out that Grimbergen is 9%. On the metro I meet some Ireland fans who are going up to Boulevard de Clichy to join what is apparently the mother and father of Irish street parties. I change trains and travel one stop in that direction before coming to my senses and going home.

***

Monday is the day we've been waiting for, Ireland against Sweden at the Stade de France. I try to ignore the Grimbergen hangover and make my way to Saint-Denis.

I get to the Stade de France where it turns out that I haven't been given a desk in the press box. I have to sit in the overflow section balancing my computer on my knees. I stew in resentment. I find the wifi doesn't work in this section and I'm forced to look around at my surroundings. Unexpectedly, I slip into a strange state of hyper-awareness. All the colours look brilliant and vivid, Irish green to the left, Swedish yellow to the right. This is how it looks just before hope gives way to reality.

Just then I hear someone calling my name. It's Raphael Honigstein, who's saying there's a free seat at his desk. I scramble over a chain link barrier and sit down next to him just as the anthems are ending.

The match kicks off and both teams start booting the ball around as though it owes them money. Nobody can get a grip on the game.

After a few minutes of robust Irish-Scandinavian football I realise that Raphael's presence is making me feel self-conscious about the team. Every time an Irish player has a bad touch I wince. I remember ten years ago he came to Dublin to see Ireland play the Czech Republic (Germany were in the qualifying group). It was Paul McShane's competitive debut and we all thought he'd done quite well, apart from getting done by Jan Koller for the Czech equaliser. When I mentioned McShane to Raphael after the match, he grimaced. "So much wrong."

Now I feel as though I am watching the school play with the parent of the confident child who is wowing the crowd in the lead role, while my child, a stranger to grace, clumps about the stage bumping into things.

Maybe he reads my mind because after a few minutes he leans over and says "So… when's the football going to start?"

Fuck you Raphi.

As though in response to his taunt Ireland finally start to play. They put together some good passing moves in midfield. Brady cuts in and hits a hard right-footed shot from the edge of the box that flies just over. Nicely struck with his weak foot. Then Hendrick smacks one off the bar from 25 yards.

Hendrick looks like he is enjoying himself. He's good with both feet and he sees the game a couple of steps ahead. By half-time even Raphael concedes that Ireland have played quite well.

The break brings Kiss Cam, where a camera picks out various types of couples around the stadium and keeps them on the big screen in a heart-shaped graphic until they bow to the pressure of the thousands cheering them on and kiss. Irish and Swedish fans kiss each other to general hilarity. They should have done this with England and Russia at the Velodrome.

Ireland score three minutes into the second half. Some goals, like Modric's yesterday, come out of nothing. This one you can feel coming from the moment Hoolahan sets Long and Walters running into the corner after a quick throw. Coleman chips in a lovely cross and Hoolahan buries it on the half volley. I pound my fist on the table. See that Raphi? Total Irish football.

But now that Ireland have the lead it's nosebleed time. Sweden get back on top with a series of corners. Ciaran Clark seems worryingly determined to score an own goal. Eventually he succeeds, heading Zlatan's driven cross past Randolph.

And then Ireland's nose magically stops bleeding and they are the better side again. In the end, the 1-1 draw feels like a bad result.

Afterwards a few of the journalists go for a drink near Gare du Nord. I'm wondering what I missed out on last night at the Boulevard de Clichy. We decide to go and see what the Irish fans are doing.

The Ireland fan experience has evolved since the *Joxer Goes To Stuttgart* era. Back then the admiring audience for good-hearted Irishness was restricted to those people who were there to see it. If Christy Moore didn't write a song about it, nobody else ever knew it had happened.

9%

12/13.06.16

Thus generations wasted their sweetness on the desert air.

Now the fans can record and instantly share their performances with a global audience, in real time and for posterity. The Irish crowd has become a self-aware superorganism with formidable media skills. For two days Irish fans have been posting thousands of videos of themselves bringing a smile to the face of Paris with their zany good humour. Every clip reinforces the same fundamental message: We Are The Craic.

It's hard to know what to make of so much craic. Something about it strikes me as needy and self-congratulatory and perhaps even obnoxious. As the Guardian journalist Barney Ronay would tweet a couple of days later: "Got out of my hotel shower this morning some Irish fans in flags and top hats making the bed and hoovering. Not sure when it becomes too much." Then we arrive at the Boulevard de Clichy to find thousands of Irish and Swedish fans have crowded the street for several hundred metres in front of the Moulin Rouge. People are drinking cans from the little convenience stores.

It doesn't feel like it's for the benefit of an audience. Everyone is just having a really good time.

ENGLAND, WALES, AND BRITAIN FIRST

(SUNDAY, MONDAY JUNE 16)

Lens is a depressed little town ringed with gigantic slag heaps, 90 minutes on the train from Paris across the flat plains of northern France. A hundred years ago this was the British sector of the Western Front. Today there are nearly 40,000 Brits in town for England v Wales.

England are heavy favourites but obviously capable, under Roy Hodgson, of losing to anybody. As one of the English journalists points out, with the slagheaps and the ceaseless rain, this place even looks like Wales.

Just before kick-off the first reports emerge of an attack on an English MP, Jo Cox. She has been taken to hospital after apparently being stabbed.

The English fans outnumber the Welsh by three to one but the Welsh are making most of the noise. During their qualifying campaign they developed a big repertoire. They run through the songbook over and over: *Men of Harlech, Can't Take My Eyes Off You, Kernkraft 400.*

On 40 minutes, Rooney gives away a free-kick almost 40 yards out. It's too far to shoot, but Gareth Bale steps up and unbelievably smashes it hard enough to beat Joe Hart.

Roy Hodgson has picked an England team without any of those Leicester City players who have just won the Premier League. The England fans are screaming for Jamie Vardy. He comes out for the second half along with Daniel Sturridge and promptly equalises.

During the second half the news comes through that Jo Cox has died, and that the killer shouted something about "Britain First" as he attacked her.

In the last minute Daniel Sturridge starts and finishes a clever move to score the winner. England are through and Roy Hodgson has got away with it.

I get a lift back to Paris with one of the Irish journalists who is going back to Versaille. We talk about how we got to the point where a deranged fascist assassinates a politician on a suburban street in England?

He drops me off in the northern suburbs near the Stade de France, where Germany are at this moment playing Poland. It's a bit like walking past a house at night and seeing the lights of the TV flickering through the curtains. The flying ring that crowns the stadium is lit up beautifully under the darkening sky, but judging by the noises from the crowd it's not a very exciting game.

There's something eerie about hearing the combined voices of thousands of unseen people yet to be walking down streets which are deserted except for groups of armed police. I feel alone and apprehensive.

It must have looked like this last November on the night the bombers blew themselves up at the gates? All these policemen are here to stop anything like that from happening again but the sight of them doesn't reassure, it just adds to the vague

sense of brooding menace.

I get on the train and stand near the door. An American couple stand nearby. I notice a man of Arabic appearance who is acting strangely. He is stooped over against the door with his forehead buried in his forearm, I think I can hear him moaning. Is he tired? Is he sick? Obviously I don't express any concern, this is public transport.

We stop at Gare du Nord and this man straightens up and gets off the train. On the floor beside where he was standing I can now see there is a backpack. I look at the backpack, then out the door after the guy, then look around to see if anyone else has noticed. The American man is looking back at me and we know we are both thinking the same thing.

He picks up the backpack and lobs it straight out through the open door of the train. I watch in horror as it sails through the air - and lands on the platform with a soft cloth impact. "Better safe than sorry," says the American. I'm not sure that hurling the backpack away was the wisest thing to do if our suspicions about it had been accurate, but there's no point getting into it at this stage.

Moments later a ragged-looking guy comes up the carriage, looking for something on the ground. He mentions a "sac". Someone points to the backpack lying on the platform and he is able to retrieve it before the door closes.

I make my way home, trying not to racially profile any more of my fellow passengers.

16.06.16

A BELGIAN RECKONING

(JUNE 17/18)

Next day is the four-hour train to Bordeaux for Ireland versus Belgium.

Marc Wilmots and Thibaut Courtois are doing Belgium's Match Day Minus One press conference. Things are supposedly tense between them because Courtois walked off the field after they lost to Italy and trashed Wilmots' tactics in a series of interviews. It was reported that they'd later had a stand-up row that nearly came to blows.

The Belgian journalists aren't sure if this is true but when the two of them come in and sit down, their mutual dislike is plain to see. Wilmots presses his thin lips together and glares at the journalists with loathing.

They respond with some light baiting. Someone asks him if it's true that some of his players call him "Moi, Je" (Me, I) in mockery of his apparent habit of talking about himself all the time. He says it's not true. Maybe they should have asked Courtois.

A couple of hours later Martin O'Neill and John O'Shea couldn't be more different. They are a relaxed comedy double-act. It's all "Oh, that's a tricky one, I think I'll leave it to John!" and "Oh I don't know,

what do you think, Boss?" with exaggerated side-eye.

We Irish journalists troop back to the media centre and file optimistic preview pieces concern-trolling the poisonous atmosphere in the Belgian camp.

There are a lot of Irish fans in the centre of Bordeaux later that night and it's a bit messy. A crowd of them are in the square kicking a football around. They see a couple of girls in a second story window and start shouting up at them. They are cheering whenever the girls stand in the window or wave, and booing whenever they go back into the room. It's a copy of a scene in Paris that almost every Irish fan in France has already seen, when a crowd of them did the same thing with some old guy on his balcony in Paris. The crowd is getting more advanced all the time but they still have to learn each trick can only look spontaneous once.

***

Saturday is game day. We are primed and ready to hit Belgium right on the point of their massive glass jaw. They've got the skills, but we've got the harmony. After ten minutes we're getting a harsh reminder that skills are more

important than harmony. Belgium are making Ireland look like training cones. Playing against us was just the tonic they needed to remember why they once fell in love with the game.

By some miracle it's still 0-0 at half-time. A chance to regroup and disrupt the dangerous patterns. The second half opens a bit like Sweden, with Ireland pushing on. We get a free kick, the ball is sent into the box. Alderweireld and Vermaelen combine to drop-kick Shane Long in the head. It's a clear penalty but play goes on. The injustice rattles Ireland, breaks their concentration. The Belgians tear down the right, James McCarthy misses a tackle, de Bruyne finds Lukaku and it's 1-0.

This is not good. Hazard, Lukaku and De Bruyne are the most ruthless flat-track bullies in Europe. They're in full flight. The Irish team is nothing more than a loose disorganisation of yawning gaps. McCarthy loses Witsel who scores the second with a towering, unmarked header. Lukaku scores again when Clark rushes out and fails in an attempt to chop down Eden Hazard on halfway. The Belgian fans gloat and bounce. Well, that was conclusive. We are shit and we are probably going home.

18.06.16

DON'T TAKE ME HOME

(JUNE 20/21/22)

On Monday it's down to Saint-Etienne for England v Slovakia. It's an unlovely town but a beautiful stadium.

Since England are already through, Roy Hodgson has decided to use this game to have a look at the options on the bench. He's made six changes to the team. The England fans don't like the decision to rest Wayne Rooney. Whenever the captain goes out to the sideline to warm up there is a huge chorus of "ROONEH, ROONEH!" Roy can do without this.

But when Rooney comes on he can't do anything. It's one of those tournament dead rubbers where the draw suits both teams. Neither side wants to take a risk. The draw means England finish second in the group and they will play Iceland in the second round. I think it's worked out nicely for them.

But the English journalists are tetchy. They've been down this road before and they are filled with nameless foreboding. They don't understand why Hodgson made so many changes - what about the all-important rhythm? With a flash of irritation, Hodgson retorts that England have played fantastic football and if they keep playing like this, it won't be long before some unfortunate opponent gets a damn good thrashing.

***

Tuesday 21st is Northern Ireland v Germany at the Parc des Princes. The Northern Irish fans are even louder than the Welsh, though their repertoire is smaller. Their feverish renditions of their Will Grigg song border on collective mania. It couldn't be more obvious that they are calling us out, they want to take

our title as Europe's Kings of Craic.

If you want to take the crown, I think smugly to myself, you might need to decommission the old *Ten German Bombers* song. Then again, there aren't many countries whose every song is unimpeachably politically correct. The Germans remain obstinately fond of their rhythmic *Sieg!* chant, which always gets an airing at tournaments, despite its disreputable overtones.

Germany dominate the game to an almost ridiculous degree but their finishing is tame. Northern Ireland's keeper Michael McGovern makes seven saves to keep the score down to 1-0.

Afterwards I watch the Ireland press conference from Lille on the UEFA site. Seamus Coleman is the captain, John O'Shea mustn't be playing. Coleman has already mastered the laconic tone of the classic, steely, incredibly boring captain. He makes Robbie Keane sound like David Norris.

Lille turns out to be a magnificent city, though it looks more like Belgium or Holland than France. They were expecting rain so they've closed the stadium roof, but it's turned out to be a hot day and you suspect the place is going to be stinking.

In the media centre everyone is watching an extremely funny game between Portugal and Hungary. Ronaldo keeps scoring brilliant goals and throwing ridiculous tantrums.

The Irish XI drops an hour before the game and it's a big surprise. O'Shea, Clark, Whelan and Hoolahan are out; Duffy, Keogh, McClean and Murphy are in. The team is full of big, strong, tall, tattooed players. It

looks like Martin O'Neill wants to find out whether Italy like it up 'em.

Everyone expected Antonio Conte to rest players, and he has made eight changes. But he was never expecting Ireland's team to look like this.

Ireland hit Italy hard from the outset but the referee keeps the cards in his pocket. As usual the problem is that Ireland can't score. Bernardeschi shoves over McClean in the box for a blatant penalty but the referee doesn't see it.

In the second half, Lorenzo Insigne comes on for Italy and three minutes later he hits the post with a curling shot.

Then, out of nothing, Ireland have a chance to win the match. Italy's captain Bonucci falls over inexplicably 25 yards out and Hoolahan pounces on the ball. He's in, advancing into the box with only Sirigu to beat. He can score in any one of about 20 ways but it's as though, confronted with so many possibilities, his brain averages them all out. The shot goes straight at the goalkeeper.

That's it. We know we will not get another chance as good as that. And for Hoolahan to be the one who wasted it, Hoolahan who was ignored for so long, and fought his way to the top at the age of 34, only to be the one who is guilty of the miss that will be remembered forever.

And as we're all grieving for Hoolahan, Robbie Brady is passing it forward and starting a run from his own half. Aiden McGeady takes it forward a few yards as Brady runs past him in the centre. McGeady gives it to Hoolahan in the right

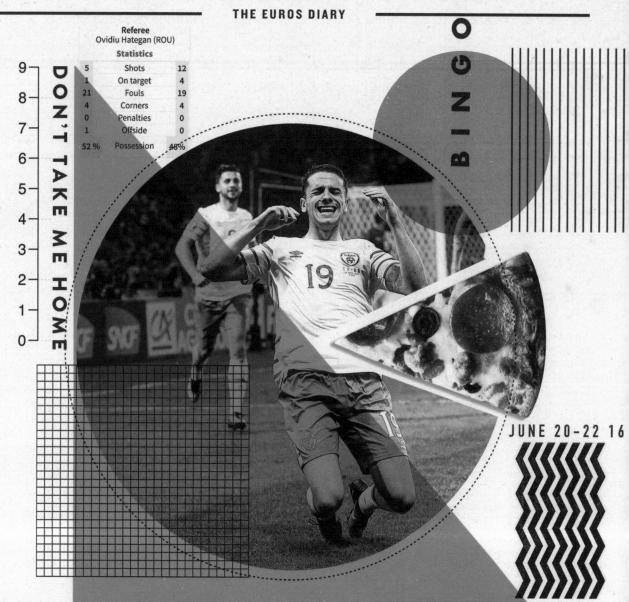

BINGO

DON'T TAKE ME HOME

Referee Ovidiu Hategan (ROU) Statistics		
5	Shots	12
1	On target	4
21	Fouls	19
4	Corners	4
0	Penalties	0
1	Offside	0
52 %	Possession	48%

JUNE 20-22 16

channel. He checks back onto his left foot and whips a diagonal cross towards the penalty spot. The ball curves into Italy's box in a beautiful redemptive arc, dropping perfectly for Brady to head it on the run past the stranded Sirigu.

It's one of those moments when the steady flow of reality breaks up. It feels like the stadium is shaking as the Ireland fans behind the goal go crazy. There are lapses of propriety in the press box as we leap up screaming and hugging each other. We're vaguely conscious of Brady and the rest of the Irish players piling into a heap on the far side of the stadium. Later we see the incredible photograph of Brady, his girlfriend and his ecstatically weeping brother, which, Martyn Rosney points out, is composed like

a Renaissance masterpiece.

Ireland will go on to Lyon to play against the hosts. UEFA's schedule means that France seem to have been preparing for this game their whole lives, while Ireland will barely have the chance to shower and change before it's time to go again. Right now nobody cares: for the team, it's mission accomplished.

Ireland mixed zones are always much better after they have won. Even James "water off a duck's back" McCarthy talks for nearly fifteen minutes. He's relieved, he knew he needed the performance he put in tonight. Jeff Hendrick has a pizza in one hand and a beer in the other and is trying to explain why a guy who just dominated midfield against Italy has been struggling to

get into the team at Derby. He gives the impression it's a bit of a mystery to him too.

You might expect that after a win like that the fans would party till dawn. But two hours after the game, central Lille is dead. There are only occasional groups of stragglers, many of them sitting exhausted on the ground. The fountains that earlier were bubbling with suds are still and stagnant. Everyone is spent.

I ask a friend who's been in France since the beginning if he's going to stay on the extra few days for the game in Lyon. He stares at me with the haggard blood-rimmed eyes of a man who has been drinking for two solid weeks. "You must be fucking joking."

BREXIT

The next day is the 23rd of June, the day of the Brexit referendum. I haven't paid it much attention. I've assumed they'll vote Remain, because the Leave campaign is led by obvious frauds and chancers whose arguments are either deceitful or moronic.

I'm tired after a busy few days and don't feel like staying up to watch the count live. Shortly before midnight I look at Twitter and see that the odds on Leave have lengthened to around 8/1, which settles it in my head. I tweet a couple of penetrating insights about how Brexit was a stupid idea anyway and go to bed.

The next morning I'm woken early by the buzz of my phone getting a message. I try to go back to sleep but then there's another buzz, and another, too many messages for this time in the morning. I crawl out of bed to take a look.

So they've voted to Leave. David Cameron has already resigned. Nigel Farage has been on morning TV admitting that his campaign lied but it doesn't matter now because Britain has seized back her independence from the junta in Brussels.

It's an outcome of stunning stupidity and for the rest of the day it's impossible to think about anything else.

The subject comes up in the Euros podcast. I babble about how I feel sorry for the Remainers who will lose the right to live and work wherever they want in the rest of the EU.

Later I see that I've always thought of those rights as things I can use to my advantage. Many Leave voters think of them as things others can exploit to their disadvantage.

The Remain case was boring. Economic arguments few people understand and fewer relate to. The Leave case was emotional: take back control. Control of what? Who cares - fuck you.

An emotional case for Remain could have reminded people of the founding idealism of the European project. It's always been political more than it is economic. European integration is all about peace.

But peace only seems exciting to people who remember what war is like. And there aren't many of those left in England, or in Europe. All the energy was on the fuck-you side.

In America the fuck-you candidate is running on a program of nationalism and protectionism straight out of the 1930s. I didn't think he could win either. Now, for the first time, I can see that he might.

James McClean tweets a picture of himself and Martin McGuinness with the message "Reignition of the flames of reunification. #BorderPoll #UnitedIreland". "Flames", nice one James. Within a couple of hours he has deleted his account.

***

Simon Kuper writes that weekend that watching the England crowd is like "looking into the dark Europe-hating id of the Brexit campaign."

It's true that the England crowd gets involved in more trouble than fans from anywhere else, but why is that? Is there any obvious difference between them and any other group of fans? One difference is that fans from the other big countries - France, Germany, Italy, Spain - don't stake out territories and mass in big groups to sing and drink like the English do. They walk around in threes and fours. They're not really a crowd in the same sense, just people wearing the same shirts.

The England crowd is male-dominated and macho, with shirtless steroid-inflated musclemen replacing the shirtless beer-bellied hardmen of the past. For all the riotous disorder that erupted around their fans in Marseille, you could also sense a powerful conformism, a submission to a traditional idea of what lads on tour should be getting up to, as though it were completely obvious that being a real fan is all about jumping up and down bumping against each other and spilling beer on each other's muscles.

The behaviour of the Irish fans is like the English in that lots of them gather together in the same place. And both the Irish and the English actively try to get the attention of the locals, which you don't see happening so much with other supporters. But they do it in quite different ways.

The Irish fans, with their ostentatious efforts to charm, are obviously trying to please. They want to be liked. They want the French, and whoever else might be watching, to think they are a great bunch of lads.

The English fans are the opposite. When they direct a song at a squad of French policemen, it's not some suck-up ironic chant like "Shoes Off for the French Police." It's more likely to be "Fuck Off Europe". They genuinely could not care less what a bunch of foreigners thought of them. They seem to enjoy being disliked. If they're in some foreign city and they're pissing everybody off, then that's good because it means they must be doing things on their terms. "Marseille Is Ours."

Needless to say, there are plenty of England fans who go about quietly with their friends and would be happy to sing along to *Dancing Queen* with the post-masculine Irish and Swedes. Maybe the split is about 52-48?

England will play the winner of the Ireland-France game in Paris. England-Ireland would be huge, but I think now I'd rather it didn't happen.

***

In the Lyon media centre before Ireland play France one of the journalists says: I think this Brexit shit has ruined the tournament for me. Well, he's American. Robbie Brady's goal meant nothing to him. But I can see his point. For a couple of days now every time I've spoken to a French person, they have assumed I'm English and said how sorry they feel for me. There's nothing patronising about their sympathy, everyone genuinely seems mystified. Tom Ewing describes the vote in New York magazine as: "a national

devaluation — not just of the pound, but of Britain itself — as the markets adjust to our new reality as a small, rainy island, which doesn't manufacture much and just told its friends to fuck off."

With due respect for Eurovision, the Euros are the closest thing Europe has to a festival of itself that people actually enjoy. This tournament brings the illusion of a united and peaceful Europe to life.

Before every game they play a song by David Guetta and Zara Larsson, This One's For You. "We're in... this... together! Hear our hearts... beat... together! We stand... strong... together!" etc. Turns out Guetta and Larsson don't know what they're talking about.

With the unexpected violence between the fans and now this Brexit shitshow, the illusion has lost its power - it seems artificial, or beside the point.

The Europarty has started to feel like a dysfunctional family barbecue, at which your aunt and uncle have just had a big fight and announced they are getting divorced.

That said, for the time being Ireland are still at this barbecue and wondering what would happen if they discreetly opened another bottle of wine.

DON'T LET THE DOOR HIT YOU ON THE WAY OUT

(JUNE 26/27)

The new stadium at Lyon is probably the best of the tournament venues. 55,000 French fans make a sea of fluttering tricolours. They must hand out free flags. It looks good but you can tell it's just for show. A mime of patriotism because that's what you do at a match. The days are gone when the French got really into this flag-waving business. It's probably better this way than the old way.

Ireland kick off and play a smooth series of passes. Stephen Ward makes a burst up the left, crosses, and Paul Pogba barges over Shane Long in the box. Incredibly, the referee whistles for a penalty. Robbie Brady nails it in off the post, France 0-1 Ireland after four minutes.

Can this seriously be about to happen? Is it possible we can survive an 86-minute nosebleed?

At half-time the French go into their dressing room, scream at each other, and come back out with a new attitude. Antoine Griezmann was on the right wing for much of the first half but now he's in the middle trying to link with Olivier Giroud.

Griezmann is a little guy but he knows how to time a jump. He gets his head to Sagna's cross and it's 1-1. Now the big stadium is really behind the French team. Then Giroud dominates Keogh in the air and lays it off. Griezmann's control is immaculate and his finish is devastating.

Ireland are like mountain climbers who have run out of oxygen. Players are cramping up. Even Coleman looks like he's trying to run on wooden legs. We all know it's over well before Shane Duffy gets sent off for the professional foul that

denies Griezmann his hat trick. Some of the Irish players cry on the field, but part of every one of them will be glad this thing is over.

It seems natural to fans that players ought to love tournaments. We see our first one as a child and playing in one - for your country! - looks like the most fun anyone could ever have.

But for a lot of grown-up players, international tournaments are a pain in the arse. For most of them, a tournament is having to go away for six or seven weeks on a work trip with a large group of people you don't really like.

Either you play, in which case you are under insane levels of pressure and scrutiny, and will probably end up with all kinds of people you've never even met insulting you in your home country's media. Or you don't play, in which case the whole thing is purgatory for the ego in addition to being a massive waste of time. Then your team loses, and almost immediately it's time to go back for pre-season training.

Spain versus Italy looked like the pick of the second round, but it doesn't turn out that way. Spain's winger, Pedro, has been moaning about how boring it is to be an unused member of the squad. I suspect his sentiments are shared even by a few of the players who are getting picked.

Spain have won two Euros and a World Cup. Three times they have been to the Promised Land. Now they'd rather go to Ibiza, or Dubai, anywhere but the Promised Land again. Goals by Chiellini and Pelle allow Spain to clock off and go home.

I hurry back into town to catch England v Iceland with a couple of friends in the Latin quarter. I arrive just as Iceland are scoring their second goal. This match is going to be more interesting than I thought.

We drink many carafes of cheap red wine and engage in much cheap laughter at England's expense. I can't remember ever laughing so hard at a football match.

I know it's not fair. All the English colleagues I know are horrified by Brexit. The England players have had nothing to do with it. Poor old Roy Hodgson is probably as Europhile as it's possible for an Englishman to be without actually being the agent of a foreign intelligence service.

But tonight England are representing the 52% and their downfall is like a little piece of cosmic justice. Don't let the door hit you on the way out.

EXIT MUSIC

(JUNE 20/21/22)

Before the quarter-finals I have dinner with a couple of English journalists. One of them says he's not worried about Brexit, but it's not because he thinks it will turn out for the best. It's because he believes that quite soon, something much worse is going to happen. The £350 million a week NHS bullshit won't seem like that big a deal when Russia invades the Baltics.

We have tournament fatigue. The best days of any tournament are in the very beginning, when everyone is still involved and anything can happen. The more teams get knocked out, the less exciting it gets. From inside the tournament bubble, you can see the outside world losing interest and moving on.

France have made the quarters and look like the best team remaining but there is still no sign of domestic Euros fever. Paris is no football city. The most excited football fans in

Paris are the local Portuguese. There are dozens of Portugal flags hanging from the apartment blocks near the Gare du Nord.

Portugal are the first team into the semis, beating Poland on penalties. Wales beat Belgium 3-1 in a classic. Germany v Italy is a 1-1 bore, notable only for a penalty shootout of astounding ineptitude, in which Germany prevail. France v Iceland is a 5-2 turkey shoot.

In the semis, France beat Germany, and Ronaldo beats Bale.

The final should be easy for France but Portugal have a mystifying rope-a-dope resilience, and it's becoming increasingly clear that destiny is on Ronaldo's side.

Destiny seems to abandon Ronaldo when he is forced off the field on a stretcher after 23 minutes. But his team-mates, led by Pepe, resist

heroically. France can't seize the moment. They don't know how to unpick Portugal's defence, and as the goallessness drags on they start to get scared. In the end they can barely muster the courage to attack at all, and Portugal win it with Eder's long-range shot.

The Portuguese are so ecstatic you feel that even the French are happy for them. They don't care enough to be really disappointed. The last time France hosted a major tournament in 1998 people genuinely believed that this shared experience had the power to change the country. This time there's been none of that. You get the sense that they're just relieved that the tournament is over and nothing terrible has happened. Four days later on the promenade in Nice, something terrible does happen. No tournament ever had a shorter afterglow.

EPILOGUE

The earliest verdict on Ireland's Euro 2016 campaign comes from Michael Cox, the tactics writer, who tweets shortly after full time in Lyon: "Ireland were poor at this tournament. Technically and physically inadequate, very fortunate to face half-arsed Italy in final group game."

It prompts an angry reaction from Ireland fans and journalists, including me. How dare this unfeeling Englishman plunge the cold steel of dispassionate analysis into the tender beating heart of Irish suffering.

Cox's timing could be better. And the first part of his point is wrong: by their own standards Ireland have not been poor at this tournament. But when it comes to the sensitive question of our technical and physical capacities, maybe we just can't handle the truth.

We always like to criticise our team for never holding on to the ball, never passing constructively, never really trying to control the game. We say all this as though whether or not we control games was a question of philosophical inclination, rather than of basic ability.

The truth is that we're not good enough to dominate games at this level. We could try a more ambitious gameplan, we could decide we were going to be "protagonists", as Guardiola says - but we wouldn't have the players to carry it through. There are only two or three players in our squad who might get picked by the teams who have made the quarter-finals.

Even the notion that we compensate for our lack of technical skill by trying harder is undermined by the running stats showing that Ireland covered only 103km per game in the group stage, less than any other team in the tournament except Albania (who had a man sent off in the first half of their first game).

But it would be boring if every analysis of the Irish team was: "We don't have enough good players, Bill." So we prefer to hold on to the illusion that we do, while being aware, at some level, of the truth.

And this inadequacy is a kind of blessing. When you know you're not good enough to expect anything, you're grateful for everything. Which is why Ireland's supporters can have fun supporting a mediocre team, while England's can't.

Sometimes people forget that for an event like the Euros, what happens on the field is a byproduct, secondary to the festival and the illusion. It's less a football competition and more a waking dream, a vision of a Europe at peace with itself.

In Poland during Euro 2012, Roy Keane talked about the Irish fans going along for the drink and the sing-song. Why complain about fans going for a drink and a sing-song when the Euros itself is really just an excuse for a drink and a sing-song?

The Ireland fans are actually the ones that get it. Thousands of Irish people went around France grinning like idiots and acting much nicer than they ever would at home. And so what?

We've got to change the mentality, Keane said. We've got to stop this idea that we're happy just to be there. But there's nothing wrong with being happy to be there. Being happy to be there is what it's all about.

Welcome to Eoin's Poems

with Eoin McDevitt!

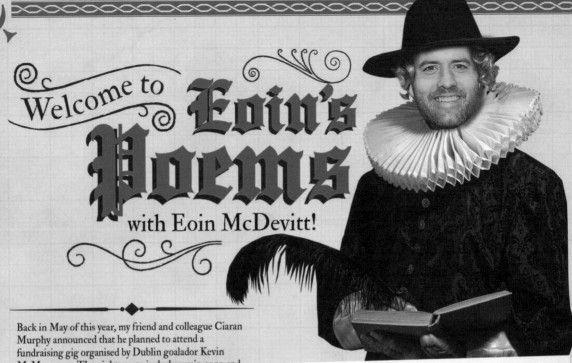

Back in May of this year, my friend and colleague Ciaran Murphy announced that he planned to attend a fundraising gig organised by Dublin goalador Kevin McManamon. The night was to include music, song and poetry. Concerned that my pal Murph would make a complete eejit out of himself by turning up empty-handed, I penned a little poem for the occasion and slipped it into his back pocket. Alas, "Anton O'Toole, Dublin's Fair Jewel" remained in that pocket all night, unread and unloved.

Unperturbed, I set about showcasing my art to the widest possible audience. And so began 'Eoin's Poems', undoubtedly the most divisive slot in the history of international podcasting. Some critics have described it as "dreadful" and "shit" while others have been staunch in their support, declaring: "I enjoy how much it annoys Ken."

Now, dear reader, the time has finally come to commit 'Eoin's Poems' to print. I have asked you to compose your tributes to the departing legend of Irish football, Robbie Keane, and I have been humbled by your response. A quick reminder, before we go on, of my rigid rhyming rules (that's some alliteration right there):

RULE 1: Four stanzas
RULE 2: Four lines per stanza
RULE 3: AAAA rhyming scheme

Sample stanza (taken from *"Anton O'Toole, Dublin's Fair Jewel"*):

The right foot was cruel
The left made your drool
From January to Yule
He was Anton O'Toole.

With those rules in mind, I invite you to enjoy four of the very best reader entries, and one of the worst. All poems are critiqued and graded by yours truly.

Yours in Poetry,

Eoin McDevitt
Chief Curator

(B-)

Untitled
By John Murphy

✻ Strong direct opener cuts straight to our hero's finest moment

I broke a nice flower pot when you slotted one past Kahn
The cartwheel celebration told the world you were the Man
Against Spain only you stayed calm - Casiellas stood still, couldn't even get a palm
We would surely have won, if it weren't for bloody Saipan

✻ A charming sentence despite its obscene length & the misspelling of the word "Casillas"

Within a few years you'd be captain – brainwave from Stan
Cyprus, San Marino and 'areas of green land'
But the Gaffer was soon gone – no Four Year Plan
Out with Drogheda, in with Milan

Trap thought we were crap, no room for Hooli-han
You were our Totti, our Muller, our Zidane.
Andews, Whelan, and Zinedine Kilbane
It was all going so well, until Henry's hand

Poland was rubbish – the team rightly panned
But at least we had Tallinn, when for once it was them who got slammed
MON-Keano arrived, and you went to Big Sam *you mean Uncle Sam?*
LA is your oyster, Ireland your land

✻ Profound closing line

CRITIQUE
You had me at "areas of green land." This poem oozes machismo and aggression, both in its style and in its content. So much so that I'm almost afraid to pull you up on your flagrant flouting of the rhyming rules in the final stanza. A tour de force.

GRADE : B-

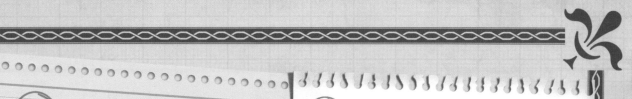

A

He, Keano
By Dave Field

Evocative title

He stormed on the scene like Il Niño,
As hot as a roast jalapeno,
Could you believe he was only seventeen? No.
But he had just finished reading the Beano.

Excellent analogy Jalapeños are extremely hot.

He cherry picked his spots like maraschino,
More often against teams like San Marino,
But you'd back him in an online casino,
This verse was endorsed by Tony Cascarino.

I don't know what this means, therefore it must be a clever line

His journey's been as long as the Camino,
And now he's sipping on a skimmed cappuccino,
With the likes of Quentin Tarantino,
In a Galaxy far from Marino…

The crowd roars like an old Gran Torino,
Or a 1990s version Al Pacino,
As we cheer on our own "Great Bambino",
And for the last time we all call for "Keano".

Gripping, tearjerking final stanza

CRITIQUE
A rip roaring, analogy packed, sometimes confusing, always amusing journey through the career of an Irish football great by a uniquely gifted writer with a penchant for pathos. Well played sir.

GRADE
A

B+

A Poem in tribute to Robbie Keane on the occasion of his retirement from International football
By Grace O'Sullivan

Extremely thorough & informative title

Robbie, as mustard he's keen
The main man of the Irish team
Many moments of brilliance we've seen
His send-off an unscripted dream

Very impressive inversion of well known phrase

His debut he made as a teen
With ambition to fulfil his dream
Pulling on that jersey of green
146 times capped he has been

seamless weaving in of career statistics

Possessed of the goal-scoring gene
68 times he scored in between
His last against Oman the cream
To honour his boys and Claudine

crowd pleasing inclusion of Ireland's favourite international friendly opponents

An Inspirational captain I mean
Who always kept his nose clean
And that's why we say Robbie Keane
For Ireland, the best ever seen

simple use of the name of the main protagonist

CRITIQUE
If I can just wipe away these tears for a moment… A truly stunning tribute here by Grace, encompassing Robbie's goalscoring prowess, leadership skills and child rearing abilities. What a man, what a poem.

GRADE
B+

F

Hai-Keano
By Ken Early

spring sunshine rises
sensini chasing helpless
fettercairn sparrow

3 line stanza?!

swift feet of summer
a hunter's bow and arrow
kashima lion

BORING…

the fox in autumn
undone like brave achilles
cruel hand of paris

This doesn't even rhyme

pacific winter
the king of angel city
just one of those things

???

CRITIQUE
Haiku? Hai snooze more like. Mr. Early blithely ignores the four-lines-per-stanza rule and seems to take a perverse sort of pleasure in subverting the AAAA rhyming scheme. If I didn't know better, I might be inclined to think the poet has a sneering disregard for the entire concept of Eoin's Poems. An abomination.

GRADE
F

A+

Untitled
By John Bligh

No title. Genius. Creates a mystique

As I filled in 'Heroes', in a workbook for my Confirmation,
A star was arising from my small sporting nation,
Was I too premature in backing this teenage sensation?
Or would time prove him to be God's finest creation?

Ballsy opening line. Throwing a bit of religion into the mix. Provocative

So I was up on the bandwagon before it departed the station,
Feeling vindicated anew by each cartwheel celebration.
While club after club he won the fans adulation,
Donning the green was his truest vocation.

Alas, doubters emerged spouting crass defamation,
"He scores meaningless goals" the banal fabrication.
Tell Iran or ze Germans, but expect consternation,
That the man tied with Muller receive such denigration.

Punchy stanza. Not afraid to stick it to the critics

And so he hangs up his boots and I feel trepidation,
Now who will score goals as we seek qualification?
But LA rejoice, no more international complication,
He retires stateside, to his deserved coronation.

CRITIQUE
A no holds barred monster of a poem. John signals his intent early by using the notoriously tricky "confirmation" as his base word for all subsequent rhymes. He meets his own challenge headon, taking down the haters with a lyrical deftness akin to a Robbie Keane penalty against Gibraltar. Top of the class.

GRADE
A+

The Fair View

Ah be the hokey! C'mere till I tell ya! It's time for an aul tale straight from true blue Dub Ken Early and all the boyos in Biddy Early's snug in Dublin's Fairview. Get up outta dat ye auld bowsie!

"Avourneen! Cead mile failte!" comes a familiar cry.

It's Biddy the charwoman looking up from her darning with a smile, beckoning me into the snug.

"Come on and sit yourself down anseo!" she says.

I peek into the snug and look around at the friendly faces. There's Fluthers McGonigle, his smile as warm and brown as an old banana. There's oul Pudser O'Toole who usually didn't have two tanners to rub together but I knew he was flush from his gig doin the voice of the Carbon Monoxide Canary for the Gas Board.

Maybe that's why next to him is parked a surprising sight - Rattigan the bookie, with the big fur coat and the sharp eyes peering out from under the white fedora hat. His shoes have a shine that'd fair scald the eyes of you and his fingers dhripping with jewels.

Before even I have the stool pulled up

I know right well what the subject of conversation was. The same subject as every day - the Dubs. Our Dubs.

"Sit down there" says Fluthers, "and help us settle a question. We know the Dubs are lookin fair unbeatable at the moment. But if you could only pick wan of them, who would it be?"

"Well the Dubs these days is a lot of mighty men, but we all know who's the mightiest of them all" says I, "and that's none other than Diarmuid Connolly."

Everyone nodded.

"Didn't I say the same thing?"

"Magic."

"Oh he's a magic man."

"A big strong man. Lovely build on him."

"I'd say he was one of the best-made fellas I ever saw."

"And a bitta divil in him."

"But dependable too. Dependable Diarmuid."

There was a moment of silence. We lifted the glasses of porter and dhrank.

A snort came from the other end of the bar.

"If the men of 23 could see youse talkin up the likes of Connolly they'd be spinning in their graves."

The speaker was the old rag and bone man, Vinny Finucane, who lost a leg fightin the staters in 22. He seldom speaks but when he does the whole place falls quiet to listen.

Supportin himself on his crutch he raised his ball o'malt to his wrinkly oul lips and took a lengthy suck.

"That pup Connolly thinks he's a real hard chaw. But he does spend hours leppin about with weights till he's blun up like a doll. If it wasn't for all that he couldn't pull the rind off a rasher. Tell me, what is it he does be at all day?"

"He's an accountant I think," says Rattigan.

"Or some class of pen pusher, no doubt. In my day the Dubs used to do real work. Every day down the coalyard The Donor Doolin would shovel ten tons of coal. That's how you get the real natural strength."

"The Donor Doolin?" someone asked.

"The Doner was the hero of the Championship of 1923. Of course in them days the final was the follyin year, so we had the 1923 final in 1924."

Biddy dhrops a pin from her darnin and it falls with a great clatther on the bar. Fluthers whipped round and warned her to whisht.

"The Dubs was up against Mayo in the final," says Vinny. "In those days them lads still came up here thinking they had a chance.

The Donor was half-forward, still grubby with the coal dust from the morning shift. And the very first time he got the ball he turned for goal. When The Donor kicked a point, it stayed kicked. The ball flew over the bar, over the stand and out of Croker altogether."

We gasped with amazement.

"The paper the next day tracked it down. The ball flew all the way to Russell Street and would you believe it landed in a baby's pram. And d'you know which baby it was was in that pram? Only the young Brendan Behan himself. That's the day he got the wonky nose. True as I'm standing here." Our eyes shone with gratitude as Vinny

continued to dispense the priceless lore.

"Well nobody had another ball. The game was suspended. But then wan of the GAA fellas had a bright idea, he was away up to Christie's greengrocers on the Clonliffe Road and a minute later he was back with a fat oul' cabbage for a ball.

"So the ref threw the cabbage in to restart the game. But when the Mayo lads got their hands on the cabbage instinct took over. They couldn't resist taking sneaky nibbles at it. Before you know it it was just an oul sprig of leaves."

> "So the ref threw the cabbage in to restart the game. But when the Mayo lads got their hands on the cabbage instinct took over. They couldn't resist taking sneaky nibbles at it. Before you know it it was just an oul sprig of leaves."

"So the ref says, we'll need something these Mayo lads won't ate before the game is over."

"And everyone was lookin around fresh out of ideas. So that's when the Donor says right, I know just the thing. And before you know it, he's taken his penknife and dug it into his belly and pulled out his own liver."

"There yis go, says he handing over the liver to the referee. That'll do yis to the end of the game, says he, turning pale and gaspin out of him. That was the love he had for the game."

"And then he slumped to the ground and there wasn't another word out of him. Now that was in the days before substitutes so the Dubs had to go on with 14 men. At first nobody could get a ghrip on the new ball but when it dried out the boys managed to sling it over the bar for a few more points.

"Well everyone knew that even though The Donor hadn't finished the game he had given as much as anyone to the cause that day. They propped him up on the bar in Sligo's of Parnell Street and gave the medal to his widow. The priest told her he'd be a true blue hero for all time. The pride of the woman, she couldn't stop crying to think of it."

"So I tell you, your Connollys and your McManamons. Is there a man among them who'd slice out his own liver for the Dubs?"

"Maybe Clucko?" suggests Fluthers.

Well Vinny flashes him a look that'd wither the face off you and from the rest of us there was only ciúnais.

But isn't it the way with every tale. Afther the laughther, the ciúnais.

Ken Early...

RIO
HEA

Michael Conlan travelled to Brazil this summer with one aim in mind: to take home a gold medal that would put the finishing touch to a glorious amateur career. He arrived home with nothing but a wounding sense of injustice and the sympathy of a worldwide audience. As the dust settles, and he prepares to start a new life as a professional fighter with Top Rank, Conlan sits down with Eoin McDevitt to work through the wreckage of his own Olympic dream and that of the Irish boxing team in Rio.

RTBREAK

There were more than a few tears shed outside the Riocentro Pavilion 6 arena. "I came out and Shauna grabbed me and hugged me and I cried a wee bit and then I stopped crying because she was crying, and there was tears in Jamie's eyes, there was tears in Paddy Barnes' da's eyes, there was tears in Paddy's eyes, and I was crying. So I just stopped crying and I says, 'Listen, it's done, there's nothing else we can do, it's over.' And they were saying, 'It's a disgrace, it's a disgrace,' so I felt I

just needed to be strong for them. Just seeing my kid running about the place, laughing, I just had to laugh. There was nothing else I could do."

Michael Conlan sits in the front room of his house in North Belfast on a quiet Thursday morning, trying to make sense of it all. This he does out of politeness for his guest, as opposed to any burning desire on his part to purge himself of the memories of Rio. "I've been trying not to think about it. I think I need to just sit

down with myself and think about it and go over it and just look at everything that I've done and look at my performance and if I truly believe that it should be behind me, it will be behind me but y'know, I haven't sat down and thought like that yet."

Instead, the weeks since Rio have been filled with the business of getting on with his life. A recent trip to the dentist sounds like it could only be matched in misery by having to attend the AIBA

41

like 'No!' and then we were like 'No!' and then they contacted the IABA (Irish Athletic Boxing Association) and got us into the airport hotel, which was far nicer." Not a great start, but much worse was to come.

Conlan remembers sitting on the balcony of his room in the Olympic Village. He was watching the draw for the boxing tournament with Paddy Barnes and Steven Donnelly when a tweet popped up about an Irish boxer failing a drugs test. As more and more tweets came through, their initial disbelief gave way to a growing anxiety.

"Everybody was worried, everybody was worried. I think everybody knew 'it's not me' but 'it possibly could be me if I've fuckin' took something wrong here. If I've took something that had something in it that's been contaminated.' We knew it wasn't us but there was always the chance, if you know what I mean."

Conlan made his way into his bedroom to call Shauna and tell her the news. As he listened to her reassurances that he had nothing to worry about, Michael O'Reilly walked into the room. "And I says to Shauna, 'I'll ring you back,' because I knew he was gonna say it." Conlan didn't have to wait long for O'Reilly to tell him, "Yeah it was me."

O'Reilly explained to Conlan that he'd failed the test, but said he didn't know what he had taken. Conlan says he asked, "Was it a shake or something, did you know what you've took?" O'Reilly replied, "Nah, I don't know. I've taken shakes and stuff but I don't know what it is." The best part of a week went by before O'Reilly publicly admitted that he "unintentionally took a supplement that may have contained a prohibited substance."

Conlan is far from happy with how the O'Reilly controversy played out. "Pat Ryan told him to stay, I don't care about saying it now. Pat Ryan told him to stay in the village. He should've been gone, in fairness, because once you fail a test, no matter what happened, if it came out he was clean, there was no way he was able to compete in the Games. He should've been gone from the start and he was told to stay by his coach who is the President of the IABA which made the IABA look like eejits because they weren't really taking any action with what was going on. I think Pat Ryan handled his case terribly."

What was Conlan's problem with O'Reilly staying on in Rio? "Because it

judges' Christmas party. There's a minor disagreement with the guy who cuts his grass to be sorted, "He just came and told me I owe him ninety quid. I don't think he's cut my grass six times since I've been away to Rio." And it sounds like there's a bit of a backlog of work to catch up on in the devoted fiancé/young father department: "When I was in training I was led like a prince, I didn't have to do anything, Shauna done everything and it was brilliant, but now I'm back to daddy duties and cleaning duties and stuff so it is hard to get used to."

Those daddy duties continue this morning as 18-month-old Luisne sits in on our interview. Michael had taken her to Brazil so that she could share in his greatest moment. A glittering amateur career had already delivered an Olympic bronze medal, a Commonwealth gold and a European gold, before he became Ireland's first ever male World Champion in Doha last October. He travelled to Rio with complete conviction that an Olympic gold medal would complete the set. You know how it ended, but let's go back to where it began.

The Irish boxing team arrived in Rio on July 20th. Their first home was a naval base that had been sourced by Billy Walsh before he left for America. It's fair to say the digs didn't quite work out. "There was no wifi which is probably one of the main things for any athlete when they go away is wifi. The beds were like you would get in the army, they were all tiny, like a prison cell. No TV in the room. The fridge had a lock on it which we

> **"I'VE BEEN TRYING NOT TO THINK ABOUT IT. I THINK I NEED TO JUST SIT DOWN WITH MYSELF AND THINK ABOUT IT AND GO OVER IT AND JUST LOOK AT EVERYTHING THAT I'VE DONE AND LOOK AT MY PERFORMANCE AND IF I TRULY BELIEVE THAT IT SHOULD BE BEHIND ME, IT WILL BE BEHIND ME BUT Y'KNOW, I HAVEN'T SAT DOWN AND THOUGHT LIKE THAT YET."**

couldn't get opened. There was an airport literally a hundred yards away so you were just hearing planes taking off every fifteen minutes. We were getting woken up at six o'clock in the morning with Red Hot Chili Peppers music and then flights started going off again after six o'clock, so it wasn't, it wasn't a nice place."

The boxers got themselves into grin-and-bear-it mode, at least until Billy Walsh landed in with his Team USA squad a couple of days later. "The Americans couldn't stay at all, they were a lot worse than us. We were like 'no' but 'we'll just get on with it, we're here for a job,' but as soon as the Americans arrived, they were was getting dragged out see, if it had've been put to an end right away and says 'right, this guy's failed a test, send him home,' it would've been finished, that would've been it. Obviously it would've been talked about still but it wouldn't have been there for a distraction for the rest of the fighters, because Michael was still about the place, he was still in the village, we were still seeing him. He wasn't out training with us or nothin' but the odd time he was coming in checking his weight and stuff because he thought he was gonna be fightin'. And I felt like saying to him, 'Listen, you are not gonna

If O'Reilly's positive test was the tsunami that engulfed Ireland's preparations in Rio, it was followed by a few more freak waves once the action got underway. Paddy Barnes beaten. Joe Ward out-brawled. Katie Taylor heartbroken. By the time Conlan stepped into the ring for his second bout he was, remarkably, the last Irish fighter standing.

Not that he was doubting himself. "People wanna have the easiest route but I wanna have a route which is gonna make me look good. And I knew I would look good against the Armenian (Aram

the blood wasn't in my eyes, there was no effect of his blood on me. I possibly could've stopped him in that round because of the way he was going back. He could've given up. It's just, it's crazy."

Conlan is prepared to accept that it was a close enough fight "at times" but "if they score the first round correctly, I've won the fight because I destroyed him in the second round. Third round was close." The loss of the first round in particular fuelled much of the national outrage at the time but, curiously, the stats tell a different story. The numbers totted up

be fighting' but I didn't wanna fuckin' break his heart obviously, but it was the truth."

Conlan doesn't dispute the notion that the whole affair added to the negative energy around the team but refuses to accept that it affected any of the performances, "Because if I'm honest, nobody gave a shit. Obviously we did care because his dream had been taken away but at the same time it's his own fault for being careless so, what can you do? There's no room for us to care. And you have to be selfish as an athlete and that's exactly what we were, we were being selfish and not giving a shit about him."

Avagyan, his opponent in the last 16). Even though I didn't perform to half my potential, I still thought I looked good against him and I knew (Vladimir) Nikitin would make me look good."
His belief was reinforced as he made his way to the ring and spotted the referee for the contest, Kheira Sidi Yakoub. "I was like, 'This is meant to be. She done my world final, she done my European final.'" But the Yakoub-Conlan success story ended abruptly in Rio. "In the second round, I gave him an absolute hiding. He was wincing, there was times in there I could hear him yelping. I hit him a shot and he stumbles back and I went to go at him and the referee stops it to clean my face of blood. I wasn't cut,

by CompuBox, the well-regarded boxing statistics provider, show that the Russian fighter landed comfortably more punches in that round, 26 shots to Conlan's 18.

"I don't see how they landed because I was gone half the time he was was throwin'. I didn't agree with the first round stats but if they done it and they analysed it, it must be that way. But it's elementary sometimes, it isn't about how much punches you do land, it's about the work that you do because you can be landing punches which you don't... like did you see his punches? They don't look like they're landing but if that was the way they scored that round, I know the next two rounds I out-landed him, so if they wanted to work it like that, I still won."

A glance at the numbers backs him up, Conlan landing 40 punches to Nikitin's 28 in Round Two, and 31 to 21 in the final round. As he stood in the centre of ring, waiting for the decision, Conlan was in no doubt that his hand was about to be raised. "I was thinking, 'There's no way they're gonna take this away from

he already had his mind fixed on quitting the amateur game. He also had a clear idea of how he wanted to bow out, "I had planned in my head that I was going to give all the judges the fingers, win or lose. But the way the fight went, it was a tough fight, the crowd was amazing, so I just says listen, there's no point doing that there, I'm finished with amateur boxing, I'll just clap the crowd and get out of here."

Michael? "Naaah, can't reveal it, it was, it was too bad but it was just so much anger towards them."

That anger poured out of him during the post-fight interview on RTÉ, eighty-five seconds of television dynamite that took this episode out of the realm of Irish sporting hard luck stories and sent it hurtling into the territory of full-on international sports scandal. Conlan

me, I'm the bloody world champion.'" And then they took it away from him. And then he reacted. An unvarnished, unscripted, volcanic reaction for sure, but one that had been lying dormant inside him for eighteen months.

You see, this isn't the first time Michael Conlan feels he's been robbed. Back in February 2015, fighting in the World Series of Boxing, he lost a contentious decision to a Kazakh fighter in Kazakhstan. At the time, he thought the defeat would be enough to scupper his plan of qualifying for the Olympics through the WSB. As he prepared for his final WSB fight, this time in Venezuela, once more against a home town fighter,

Thanks to a surprise result in another bout, that victory in Venezuela gave him enough points to qualify for Rio, where he could unleash his grand gesture of protest on the biggest stage of them all. "This time it wasn't even in my head, it wasn't planned, it just happened. And y'know, I gave them the fingers, I honestly felt like I wanted to go and grab one of them physically and just hit them... I wanted to go and physically choke one of 'em but I can't do that."

The judges did get a fair old lash of his tongue though. "When I was walking around I was was shoutin' some bad shit at them, thank god the mics didn't pick it up but it was bad." Juicy details please

attempts to put words to the emotions he was feeling: "When someone tries to take something off you that you really want, you're angry. But when someone tries to take away your dream that you've always had, and seen and felt every single day, it's hard to take and I wasn't gonna stand there and take it. I actually got people writing to me after, saying, 'Why didn't he just take it on the chin like (Vassiliy) Levit the night before, like (Erislandy) Savon in the last Olympics?' But why would I when it continues to happen? What's the point? It's not gonna change if I do that. Sit there and be a puppet and don't say nothin'."

CONTINUED ON PAGE 46

IRISH OLYMPIANS WHO TURNED PRO

Michael Conlan is never short of confidence when he's asked about the heights he can reach as a professional boxer. His answers are usually peppered with phrases like "multi-weight world champion" and "the best fighter Ireland's ever had." Catch him on a particularly good day and he might even tell you he believes he's "gonna be one of the world's best ever fighters as well." Given his outstanding record as an amateur, not to mention his burning desire to avenge the injustice of Rio, it's not difficult to see why he fancies his chances. But will it be that straightforward? As Conlan sets off on the journey, we take a look at five Irish Olympians who've travelled that road before.

WAYNE McCULLOUGH

Ireland's flag bearer at the 1988 Olympics in Seoul, and silver medallist at the 1992 Games in Barcelona, McCullough wasted little time in climbing the summit of the professional game. In July 1995, in just his seventeenth fight, the "Pocket Rocket" travelled to Nagoya, Japan to wrestle the WBC World bantamweight title from Yasuei Yakushiji. Though his career never quite touched those heights again, it's hard to argue with the legacy of a man who went the distance with two of the greatest fighters of his era, Prince Naseem Hamed and Erik Morales.

Professional Record: Wins 27 Losses 7 Draws 0

JOHN JOE NEVIN

Overshadowed a little by Katie Taylor's heroics, John Joe Nevin produced a series of dazzling displays on his way to winning a silver medal at the London Olympics. He's had to fight the majority of his professional fights with the not inconsiderable handicap of a 4lb metal bar in his leg, the legacy of a local dispute in Mullingar two and a half years ago that left him with two broken legs. The metal bar was only removed in January 2016, leading to a further lengthy period of inactivity. He got back in the ring on August 26th to record his eighth victory of a stop-start career.

Professional Record*: Wins 8 Losses 0 Draws 0 *still active

ANDY LEE

Ireland's only boxer at the 2004 Games, Lee's second round exit was scant reward for an impressive amateur career that had delivered a bronze medal at the European Championships and a silver at the World Juniors. Guided through his early years as a pro by Hall of Fame trainer Emanuel Steward, Lee was stopped by Julio Cesar Chavez Jr in his first attempt at claiming a world title in the summer of 2012. Redemption arrived in the run-up to Christmas 2014, when the Limerick middleweight stunned the unbeaten Russian Matt Korobov to claim the WBO belt on a glorious night in Las Vegas.

Professional Record*: Wins 34 Losses 3 Draws 1 *still active

MICHAEL CARRUTH

Despite Ireland's storied boxing history at the Olympic Games, Carruth's victory over Cuban superstar Juan Hernandez Sierra in Barcelona remains the one and only time an Irish man has taken home a gold medal. Professional offers flowed in from America, but he opted instead to join Frank Warren's stable in the UK and embark on what would prove to be an underwhelming pro career. His one shot at glory came in September 1997, when he made the trip to Aachen to challenge the German-based Michael Loewe for the WBO World welterweight title, only to drop a majority decision. He fought sporadically enough over the next couple of years, before retiring in April 2000 after just 21 fights.

Professional Record: Wins 18 Losses 3 Draws 0

BARRY McGUIGAN

McGuigan's professional exploits are well-documented, most notably his dethroning of the legendary WBA World featherweight champ Eusebio Pedroza at Loftus Road in 1985. Five years earlier, he had represented Ireland at the 1980 Olympics where he was beaten by a Zambian opponent in his second fight, a bout he felt he won clearly. McGuigan's autobiography contains some dark mutterings about goings-on in Moscow, "There were stories about corruption and Iron Curtain countries doing each other favours: one particularly colourful suggestion was that they were putting rat shit in the foreign athletes' food."

Professional Record: Wins 32 Losses 3 Draws 0

CONTINUED FROM PAGE 44

He remembers speaking to the print journalists and feeling himself welling up when the conversation turned to his family. So he grabbed his face, covered his eyes and escaped to the sanctuary of the changing room. "I just let a big fuckin' roar out and had my head in the towel and was just cryin' for a few minutes, and then I took my head up and I says, 'Was it that bad?' And everybody around me was saying it was bad. Uzbek coaches were coming over to me, Cuban coaches were coming over, the Cuban boxers, because there was a TV in the warm-up

what happened, they booed the judges as they walked out. I maybe humiliated them publicly for everybody else to see, but they did humiliate me and they've humiliated many fighters in the past."

Shortly after the conclusion of the Olympics, the governing body of amateur boxing proudly published a letter on its website under the headline, "AIBA and its President Dr Ching-Kuo Wu praised by International Olympic Committee President Thomas Bach for remarkable success of the Boxing

Tournament at the XXXI Olympiad Rio de Janeiro." If getting called out as "cheating bastards" by one of your sport's biggest stars and subsequently banishing a number of judges and referees can be described as a "remarkable success", one shudders to think what a "spectacular failure" might look like.

Conlan has his own take on Dr Wu's performance at the Games: "The corruption runs to the top, it filters down through everybody and people might be getting sacked because he covered his

area. And they were all watching it and they were just saying, 'You won, you won, you won.'"

Not everybody was quite so supportive. AIBA president Ching-Kuo Wu warned of disciplinary action, accusing Conlan of humiliating the officials. Conlan is unrepentant. "I can't wait to see what comes my way, and I hope it comes quite soon so I can laugh at it because he's saying I can't embarrass their judges that way or humiliate them; they humiliated me in that ring. I fought my heart out and they just took it away from me and they didn't even smile, they didn't even look at me, acknowledge what had just happened. Everybody in that arena knew

> "WHEN SOMEONE TRIES TO TAKE SOMETHING OFF YOU THAT YOU REALLY WANT, YOU'RE ANGRY. BUT WHEN SOMEONE TRIES TO TAKE AWAY YOUR DREAM THAT YOU'VE ALWAYS HAD, AND SEEN AND FELT EVERY SINGLE DAY, IT'S HARD TO TAKE...

own back. And that's what I think could be happening."

Conlan's defeat put the seal on a miserable couple of weeks for the Irish boxers and their coaches in Rio. The anticipated medal haul never materialised and that failure was greeted with criticism and recriminations. In an interview with Vincent Hogan in the Irish Independent, Pete Taylor claimed, "Every one of our boxers looked tired. They all looked overtrained. And everyone could see that the tactics were poor."

I manage to get as far as the word "tired" before Conlan cuts me off, "I think that was the biggest bullshit, jealous

CONTINUED ON PAGE 48

OUTBURSTS!

GOLD: KEVIN KEEGAN - "I WOULD LOVE IT IF WE BEAT THEM"

Celebrating its 20th birthday this year, the undisputed gold standard of post-match rants caught just about everybody on the hop at the time, including Keegan's assistant Terry McDermott. "He was right as rain going into the interview," McDermott tells Martin Hardy

in a recently published book called *Touching Distance*. "He wasn't saying, "I'm going to show that bastard." We'd just won, he was in good fettle. I was more shocked than anybody."

"That bastard," of course, was Alex Ferguson, who had suggested that Leeds United would be far less motivated to beat Newcastle than they had been a couple of weeks earlier when they tried to put a dent in Manchester United's title charge. Ferguson had also expressed misgivings about Keegan's plan to bring his team to Nottingham Forest for Stuart Pearce's testimonial, given that Forest also featured in Newcastle's run-in.

Keegan was already getting worked up when Richard Keys threw in the grenade, "But that's

part and parcel of the psychology of the game, Kevin, isn't it?"

"No! When you do that, with footballers, like he said about Leeds, and when you do things like that about a man like Stuart Pearce. I've kept really quiet, but I'll tell you something, he went down in my estimation when he said that. We have not resorted to that. But I'll tell ya, you can tell him now if you're watching it, we're still fighting for this title and he's got to go to Middlesbrough and get something, and I'll tell ya, honestly, I will love it if we beat them. Love it!"

United did go to Middlesbrough and get something, a 3-0 win to be precise.

SILVER: MICHAEL CONLAN - "AIBA ARE CHEATS"

Go on, admit it, you cheered this post-fight interview more loudly than most of the actual sporting action in Rio. Evanne Ní Chuilinn's opener, "Michael, you've a lot to get off your chest after that," was all he needed. "AIBA are cheats, they're fuckin' cheats, I'll never box for AIBA again, they're cheating bastards, they're paying everybody," and so on.

It was a display of righteous anger that gave vent to the frustrations of all Irish sports fans, as we watched the last of our much-vaunted boxing team eliminated from the Olympics in hugely controversial circumstances. It's also the

kind of outburst that gets you noticed around the world, and Conlan spent most of the next few days soaking up the reaction on Twitter.

He wasn't shy about adding fuel to the fire either, hitting the jackpot with his tweet to Vladimir Putin, "Hey Vlad, how much did they charge you bro ??" Conlan tells me, "I looked at the analytics and it's over two and a half million people have seen the tweet." Mind you, he's quick to point out that he has no personal beef with the Russian President. "I don't want him to come to my door with some nukes or anything like that," he laughs.

BRONZE: LEE ELIA - "PRINT IT!"

The Chicago Cubs had just suffered a home defeat at the hands of the Dodgers, their fourteenth loss of what was turning out to be a miserable season. Their manager, Lee Elia, was asked by a reporter about the disgruntled reaction of the fans. Three minutes and forty-nine expletives later, he realised he may have gone too far.

"I'll tell you one f*ckin' thing, I hope we get f*ckin' hotter than sh*t, just to stuff it up them 3,000 f*ckin' people that show up every f*ckin' day, because if they're the real Chicago f*ckin' fans, they can kiss my f*ckin' ass right downtown and PRINT IT!"

He continued: "The motherf*ckers don't even work. That's why they're out at the f*ckin' game. They oughta go out and get a f*ckin' job and find out what it's like to go out and earn a f*ckin' living. Eighty-five percent of the f*ckin' world is working. The other fifteen percent come out here. A f*ckin' playground for the cocks*ckers." Oh dear. As recently as 2008, on the 25th anniversary of the interview, Elia told ESPN.com that barely a day goes by when he isn't reminded of his tirade. "It bothered me," Elia said. "Very, very much, especially in the beginning. I just completely embarrassed myself and was not really happy about what had happened. That's not me."

CONTINUED FROM PAGE 46

statement I've ever heard." Jealous statement? "Yeah I think he was raging he wasn't there. He obviously wanted to be in Katie's corner, Katie doesn't want him in her corner for, for reasons which is a private matter between them ones but, y'know, where has Pete been the last few years? He hasn't trained us. He's quite jealous of Zaur I believe. The way he spoke it seems that way anyway."

"I really like Pete but that statement pissed me off and I don't like it. And it's not just me, I think everybody who has read it, reporters and all who I've spoke to did not like his statement, they didn't agree with it at all and y'know I think him coming out and saying it at that time was quite wrong. I think he had no right to come out and say what he was saying."

Regarding the specific charges made by Taylor, Conlan rejects the notion that the fighters were overtrained, "I thought that was probably one of the best camps we've had. We definitely weren't overtrained, we were ripe." And the tactics? "I believe the tactics for my fights were perfect. In the first fight, I'd been waiting so long I felt tired. I was told to box on the back foot and that was the right tactics, but I felt my legs were a bit tired so I knew I could beat him at his own game, I'll go and do that myself. Paddy's tactics are the same every time, just go out and throw punches, Paddy just goes to war all the time. I thought Davy Oliver's tactics, he didn't execute them well, but they were right in his fight. Steven Donnelly's tactics were always very good. And Joe Ward, I think

> "I THINK THAT WAS THE BIGGEST BULLSHIT, JEALOUS STATEMENT I'VE EVER HEARD." JEALOUS STATEMENT? "YEAH I THINK HE WAS RAGING HE WASN'T THERE. HE OBVIOUSLY WANTED TO BE IN KATIE'S CORNER."

he let the pressure of his first Olympic Games and everything building up to it, I think that played a part with Joe, but I can't put a fault on any of their tactics because I knew their tactics going into the fight and if they had've done them, they would've won."

Taylor was especially critical of the management of Paddy Barnes' weight, telling the Independent, "In my view, Paddy almost has a case to sue the association. He's an employee of theirs, it's their responsibility to protect him. It's not just about winning medals, it's about a boxer's health. That should be the first consideration every time."

Conlan's take: "Paddy's weight was managed, Paddy was on his weight good this time but Paddy had weighed in at eight o'clock in the morning and fought three hours later, he's never done that in

his life. He had been managed. Sport NI and Sport Ireland, they had helped him on his way there, got him his food sorted, managed it, kept track of his diet and kept looking at his weight and he had come down right and in Rio he had done the weight good, probably done the weight a bit better than me. And it was just that the fight was so quick, between weigh-in and fight, he had never done that in his life."

Conlan's dad John was part of Ireland's coaching team at the Games and Michael admits to taking some of the criticism personally. "A bit. A bit. I'd say I have because you know I think it's the first trip my da has went away on he hasn't won a medal, every trip he's been to with NI and Ireland, he's won medals. So for him to come away from this trip not winning a medal, it's sad because I know how good of a coach he is, and how good of a team him and Zaur are together."

After he left the Riocentro arena on the day of the Nikitin fight, Conlan swung by his apartment in the Olympic Village, grabbed some clothes, and headed off to stay with his family. The next few days unfolded very differently to how they might have gone if he'd been left to his own devices. "I probably would've been going mental or probably sent home or something for doing something crazy," he jokes. "I probably would've went out just messing around and just being an eejit and wasting my time instead of trying to enjoy Rio."

He was thankful for their presence, even if the beaten fighter was the one consoling his loved ones more than the other way around. And as for Luisne? "I wanted her to be there to experience her daddy winning an Olympic gold medal and to look back at pictures and say, 'I was there when he done that. I was in Rio.' Now she'll look back at a different experience and she'll say, 'I was there when that was the catalyst for making my daddy become the best fighter Ireland's ever had.'"

Right now, as a muggy Belfast morning ticks into the afternoon, Luisne looks far more interested in their impending trip to the local swimming pool. I leave our greatest ever amateur boxer to his daddy duties, safe in the knowledge that we'll be hearing plenty more from Michael Conlan as he navigates the choppy waters that lie between him and greatness in the professional game.

CURB YOUR KENTHUSIASM

"KEN'S DESCRIPTION OF HIS TRAIN JOURNEY FROM ST ETIENNE TO PARIS DURING EURO 2016 WAS ONE OF THE MOST MEMORABLE SECOND CAPTAINS MOMENTS OF 2016. HIS BATTLE FOR A SEAT IN THE TGV JUNGLE REMINDED MANY OF LARRY DAVID AND WITH THIS IN MIND, CIEMAY HAS COMBINED BOTH OF THESE ANIMALS TO CREATE CURB YOUR KENTHUSIASM..."

WORDS - KEN EARLY

ILLUSTRATION - CIEMAY

I'll give you the unvarnished account of what happened will I? There was a train at like, one o clock back to Paris. I arrived at the station at St. Etienne before that train was due to go, to find utter bedlam!

Seat numbers weren't being respected. It was with an air of foreboding I went to find class 41, and as expected it already contained a tired looking English fan.

A Geordie fan, probably in his late twenties. He knew why I'd come, and I looked at him sternly and waggled my ticket and said "sorry mate, that's actually my seat"

and he said "sorry mate, we've actually just been told to sit anywhere, the seat numbers don't count".
Basically tough shit!
So I sulked around a little bit and complained and sent angry text messages to people who didn't care.

Then I thought, there's no point in just sitting here, who knows what might happen. Possession was now 100% of the law, you have to go and find someone else's seat you can take.

So I start walking along the train and in the very end carriage there were a couple of empty seats, "ahh that's interesting" …

I went along to the first empty seat I saw and tried to sit down and the England fan said "sorry mate, our friend's there". so I said "ok", moved up to the next empty seat, sat down, the guy next to it, no complaints.

Ahh, the situation seems to have changed. I am now one of the haves rather than the have nots.

Two minutes later as I suspected it might, previous owner came along and said, "sorry mate that's my seat", and I said, "sorry mate, my seat is actually voiture 12, class 41, but there's someone sitting in it so I just came and sat in this seat which was unoccupied so we're in the same boat.

and he said, "that's ridiculous, I just gone to the canteen and I got this orangina". And I go, "I know and I'm really sorry, it's really unfair, the system is a total shambles". He walked away saying the word, "Tosser".

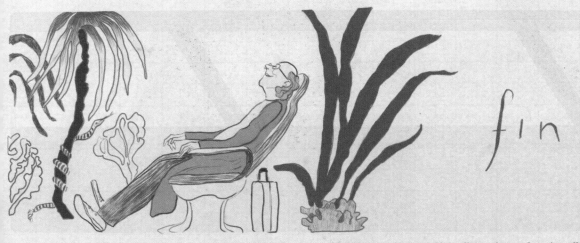

I felt bad for the guy, maybe he didn't realise he was in the jungle, he thought he was on the train but this was basically a jungle.

And I thought to myself, "well, you know, I can't really complain about that characterisation of my behaviour at this moment, however, I do have a seat and I don't think anyone saw.

fin.

THE MINOR DETAILS

Unfulfilled potential, what ifs, and if onlys – the man who 'played a bit of minor for the county' is a staple of every GAA club-house in the country. But what is it like to hit your career peak before you've finished your Leaving Cert? Murph is our man on the inside of this (not-very) exclusive club

It was a beautiful April Saturday evening in Roscommon, and I was playing for Galway in the Connacht minor league. I did ok, at full-forward. I left Dr Hyde Park in high spirits. The following morning I played a challenge game for our club minor team, and tore ligaments in my ankle. I told the county manager, I got a sympathetic phone-call about 3 weeks later to ask how I was doing, and soon after that, Galway got knocked out of the Connacht minor championship by Mayo. And that was that.

Does this get me the right side of the most prestigious velvet rope in Irish sport? Did I, in fact, 'play a bit of minor for the county'? Playing senior for your county means you've reached your limit – and you were either good enough, or you weren't. There isn't a lot of speculating left to do. The game found you out.

But to play a bit of minor for the county is the ultimate badge of honour in Irish sport. It is, in many respects, so much better than playing a bit of senior for the county, because playing a bit of minor suggests a whole ocean of unfulfilled potential, a vast reservoir of bad luck or bad decisions that meant you never went on to explore the outer limits of your ability. It basically gives you free rein to speculate on just how good you could've been.

Back in 2000 (the exact span of time which will henceforth be known as 'my day'), the idea of development squads had not gotten within shouting distance of the Galway County Board. Playing minor meant going to trials in January, surviving a few culls, attending a few training sessions, beating Mayo and getting on telly.

There was a purity to the whole process. Hard work wasn't going to get you anywhere. There was no way of skipping the queue, no way to prove yourself to be worthy of a shot by any metric other than ability. In sport, you get told all the time that God-given talent can only take you so far. In the case of the GAA, 'so far' was the county minor team. And that's the beauty of the grade. Top level sport takes sacrifice. There's no sacrifice in playing a bit of minor for the county. It's all gravy. No-one drops out, no-one just doesn't fancy it, no-one's taking a year off – if you're one of the 30 most talented footballers in your county, you're in. If you're not, well… there are no extenuating circumstances.

This is not about the guys for whom minor was an inevitable stepping-stone to the senior grade. And it's not even about the starlets who seemed destined for greatness, only to flame out spectacularly in a haze of sex, drugs, and pint bottles of cider – stay half an hour in a pub in rural Ireland and you'll hear one of those tales. It's really more about the kind of player for whom playing minor was the destination, not the starting-point; the lads who were never going to be any more than minor county men.

And every county minor team, even the very best, have 7 or 8 lads who will never play at that kind of level again. By the time the under-21 grade came along, you were cherry-picking from the best of 3 or 4 years' worth of players, so the transfer from that grade to senior was always going to be higher. But with minor? The standard of player is always a little more… representative.

I remember talking to a lad from my club who played on the Galway minor team with Padraic Joyce, Michael Donnellan, Derek Savage and the rest of the county's most gilded generation since the 1960s. Minor would always have been the aim for him, and he knew it. In the Connacht final, it was getting tight and tense in the final few minutes. By hook or by crook, my friend found himself with the ball in his hand taking a free deep inside his own half. After dithering on the ball for what seemed like an eternity, the referee appeared intent on giving a hop-ball. In a panic, and with no team-mate coming short to help him out, he drove the ball up the field blindly, with the ball going out over the side-line.

Within seconds he found himself on the wrong end of a tongue-lashing from Padraic Joyce. He meekly offered the defence that "there was no-one looking for it", to which Padraic replied – "was there someone looking for it in the fucking stand?" He doesn't even tell this story with a sigh – it's the same for all of us. He was lucky to play with people like Joyce, and the minor grade gives mere mortals the chance to do it and to represent their county while they're doing it.

Former Taoiseach Brian Cowen played minor football for Offaly, for instance. Sure, according to legend, he played on a team that lost to Kilkenny (that's the Kilkenny minor FOOTBALL team), which is an indication that this was perhaps not a minor team that would live long in the memory of the Gaels of Offaly… but he was there. He might even have sneakily held onto his jersey for posterity, and who could blame him for that, quite frankly? An image of an 18-year-old Brian Cowen doesn't automatically scream "athletic superman", but he had his moment in the sun and we should acknowledge that (along with his 8% approval rating at the time he left office).

It's the Gaelic football version of "that lad had trials with Derby…" It means, basically, nothing – but from it you can extrapolate an entire life's worth of missed opportunities. "I had potential, but of course…." And you can fill in the blanks from there.

"… but of course I lost both my legs in a horrific boating accident soon after."

"… but of course I went on to play soccer for Arsenal, Manchester City, Sunderland and my country, scoring 21 goals (Niall Quinn)"

"… but of course I went on to oversee a devastating banking bailout, and lose my dream job in disgrace (unnamed former Offaly minor footballer)"

Of course, while it's happening you're not thinking about your dim and distant future – you're all about the glorious present, and a summer rich in potential. Sure, there might be the Leaving Cert to negotiate, but there is also free county gear to wear around town ALL THE TIME. As far as a young starlet is concerned, subtlety when advertising the fact that you are on the minor panel is for idiots. Your attractiveness to the opposite sex, your status among your peers, your parents' belated pride in your achievements… these are not lights to hide under a bushel.

For those short few weeks I was in the Galway minor panel, I could sense a subtle, indefinable shift in my world view. I took pity on those poor clowns who couldn't pull themselves up by their bootstraps, get their lives together, and play 20 minutes against Roscommon in the Connacht minor league– like me. I had an almost Trumpian outlook on life. Everyone who wasn't on the Galway minor panel was a loser. SAD!

This can have a negative impact on a young man's life. You see it writ large on All-Ireland final day. There are a lot of bad haircuts on show, designed less with posterity and more with the local nightclub that evening in mind. The threat of young men losing the run of themselves in small towns like Tuam, or Thurles, or Crossmaglen, is ever-present. For this, as with innumerable other

> ## IT'S REALLY MORE ABOUT THE KIND OF PLAYER FOR WHOM PLAYING MINOR WAS THE DESTINATION, NOT THE STARTING-POINT; THE LADS WHO WERE NEVER GOING TO BE ANY MORE THAN MINOR COUNTY MEN.

things, we can blame television.

And there's no doubt about it – for many years, TV was the unspoken but nonetheless endlessly influential guiding force, the ambition tantalisingly within reach for many of the nation's young footballers. Nowadays there are minor and u-21 games on throughout the year – club games, ladies football games, Sigerson Cup games… but up until the mid-90s, there might only be 8 or 10 live Gaelic football games shown on TV, and 3 of them were guaranteed to be the two All-Ireland minor semi-finals, and the final. If you made it to the big show, you were news.

Honourable football men might go their entire careers without getting a chance to perform live in front of the RTÉ cameras. But if you were a Cork or Kerry lad, born in the 80s, one win would've gotten you there. A poxy draw and a home game against the Rossies might be enough if you were from Mayo.

Like all of my favourite ambitions, this one was within reach, and didn't take too much work. And that ambition was not simply a sporting one, not simply to play in Croke Park, but it was also to hear RTÉ commentator and gaeilgoir non pareil Micheal Ó Sé expound at length on RTÉ about whose brother/nephew/son/second cousin you were.

On and on he would drone, unintelligible for the most part to the great unwashed. But one's ears would prick up as he'd mention that the Meath corner-back was a distant relative of a name of renown from the past – you might struggle to understand the exact genealogical link, but that was unimportant. All that needed to be understood was that here was another young man who was a part of the great chain of Gaeldom. For

> ## THE THREAT OF YOUNG MEN LOSING THE RUN OF THEMSELVES IN SMALL TOWNS LIKE TUAM, OR THURLES, OR CROSSMAGLEN, IS EVER-PRESENT. FOR THIS, AS WITH INNUMERABLE OTHER THINGS, WE CAN BLAME TELEVISION.

emphasis, Ó Sé would repeat the family connection every time the young man would touch the ball, ensuring that he would almost inevitably suffer horribly by comparison.

In my childhood reveries, I saw that my uncle Jim Carney, The Sunday Game's first presenter, would get a mention when my time came – it was a tasty (some would say sexy) angle, and one sure to get me plenty of attention when we reached Croker… and yet, an angle in which my playing abilities would not be cast in an unflattering light, which might also prove to be a handy little detail.

By dint of RTÉ's rather curious decision to carry minor commentaries only in Irish (which dates all the way back to the 1960s), the grade was inextricably linked with our native tongue. I found it

hilarious that even when TV3 took over the coverage of the minor finals, they felt honour-bound to offer commentary in Irish, as if it's the unofficial language of the competition. The minor games are on TG4 now, and no better place for them.

There are much higher grades of football, of course – the under-21 grade has been for 15 or 20 years a far more reliable indicator of a lad's ability to make it at senior level. The Sigerson Cup is of a higher standard than at least 3 divisions of the National Football League at the moment. The mere idea that the minor final should be on as a curtain-raiser for the senior All-Ireland finals seems incongruous – certainly if you were drawing it up now, playing the camogie and ladies football finals before the men's equivalent would make a lot more sense, and send a hugely positive message to female sportspeople in Ireland.

But the glamour of it remains, and it is of course bound up in being 18. Is there a headier year in anyone's life? Everything is felt a little more deeply, and that includes football. While I was writing the most exquisitely awful poetry about playing corner-forward for the Milltown senior team, anything seemed tantalisingly within reach. At 18, football is still in perfect concert with the rest of your life. Soon you'll go to college and realise there are better ways to spend your time, and then you get a job, and you realise that maybe you were right when you were 18. But either way, life gets complicated. At 18, those complications don't exist. And in dimly-lit pubs, in dimly-lit towns all over the country, there are men who can proudly say that when their county came calling, they went there, they came home, and they over-wore the t-shirt.

MINOR WARDROBE ALTERATIONS
THE GEAR THAT LETS THE WORLD KNOW YOU'RE KIND OF A BIG DEAL

Socks and shorts – this is your gateway swag. They are certainly worthwhile, but they can be difficult to work into your everyday wardrobe. On the other hand, you will wear them at club training for the rest of your life, to remind everyone that you did indeed once play a bit of minor for the county. Provided your club colours are different from your county colours, you can also wear them in club league games for a couple of years afterwards, to ensure that people from opposing clubs are made aware of your fearsome pedigree.

Gear-bag – if you get this before the school year finishes, then you're on the pig's back. Throw out that bag that's faithfully seen you through the first 4 years and 11 months of your secondary school life, and get the word out there. Particularly if you ride the school bus – you can leave it there on the luggage rack, for the entire village to admire/covet.

Polo shirt – this is the key arrival in your in-box. "What's this? Oh, just my county minor polo training shirt. Free to those who can afford it… very expensive for those who can't." There are people who would tell you that it's impolite to endlessly wear your polo shirt to the local niteclub in a shameless attempt to impress the opposite sex. Those people are idiots, and don't listen to them. What's the point in doing all that training if you can't tell the world about your success? There are past graduates of the minor grade who would happily wait bare-chested by the dryer for their free polo shirt to be ready to wear again, rather than change out of it, for the duration of their summer in the spotlight.

Track-suit bottoms – now we're talking! If you intend lazing around the square in your home town for a summer, then quite frankly there's no need to ever take these bad boys off. The only slight concern is that the county crest can be a little hard to distinguish… but if you're wearing them EVERY day, then people are bound to connect the dots eventually. The county togs will do as a substitute on those rare days that call for shorts…

Jersey – the pièce de résistance, as the French would say. Keep swapping while the going's good, but when your championship run finally ends, remember to hold onto your own jersey. When the memories (and the colours in your cheaply-made polo shirt) fade, it'll do your heart good to see the jersey… just don't turn it over to reveal the number 29 on the back.

Congratulations!

YOUR SUCCESS WITH THE HOLY CONCEPTION DREADNOTS HAS NOT GONE UN-NOTICED — YOU HAVE BEEN HEAD-HUNTED BY THE FREEDONIA FEDERATION OF SOCCER PRESIDENT — YOU ARE THEIR NEW CHIEF EXECUTIVE!!

YOUR FIRST TRIP TO FIFI

VOMITORIUM →
WINE LAKE

" THE WINE LAKE IS WHERE WE DECIDE WHERE TO PLAY THE WORLD CUP... "

" WHO 'S FOR A SECOND DINNER ? "

MR WEINER MAKES A GOOD EARLY IMPRESSION

WHAT ABOUT JIMMY NESBITT TO PRESENT THE GOLDEN BALLOON?

" HE CALLS HIM JIMMY, THEY MUST BE ON GOOD TERMS. "

FIFI ARE HAVING AN ELECTION CAMPAIGN

THE INCUMBENT

THELONIOUS L HUGNAFEL

DO YOU SUPPORT THE INCUMBENT, OR THE REFORM CANDIDATE FROM THE FEDERATED STATES OF MICRONESIA, THELONIOUS L. HUGNAFEL?

DO YOU

A. YOU PICKED THELONIOUS L HUGNAFEL?

GO TO PAGE 35

B. YOU PICKED THE INCUMBENT?

GO TO PAGE 69

OUR 5-POINT PLAN TO GOING VIRAL IN 2016!

Always Be Recording – under no circumstances try and enjoy the moment as it's happening. Get your phone out and record everything that happens to you – if you're at the Euros with 30,000 other Irish people there's probably something #viral happening somewhere in your line of vision. If you spent longer than half an hour in France, be advised that you're the star of at least 3,672 youtube clips. If it wasn't for our innate goodness as a nation, you'd nearly be convinced the only reason there was no fan trouble was because the position of every single Irish fan in France, for their entire time in the country, could be very easily triangulated by the French police via Youtube.

You can never be TOO Irish – if you're an Olympic competitor, be advised – it's not just Irish content aggregators on the look-out for wacky five rings-related nonsense. You've got a global audience. So if you've got one week to appeal to the most hackneyed of Irish stereotypes, put h's where there are none, ignore the h's that are there, mention spuds a few times, and the world's your oyster. And if that's who you really are, well then all the better. Down-home country charm and nonsense are where the clicks are at. "You'll never guess what they've said next" CLICKCLICKCLICKCLICKCLICKCLICK

Incorporate props – kicking a ball through the open window of a French person's apartment is petty vandalism. Kicking a ball into a French person's apartment while wearing a horse's head is the greatest achievement by an Irish sportsperson on foreign soil since Ronnie Delany swept to gold in the 1500m in Melbourne in 1956.

Fake Sheikh-News Of The World-style surreptitious recording of your own family – watching a GAA game at home? Have a parent prone to anxiety attacks/profanity-laced arguments with the television/severe anger-management issues? Well then piggyback their mental torment to fame and fortune. They just see you tapping away on your phone, as always, they don't know you're recording. And it's not like they're ever on the internet or anything, it's the perfect crime! "Hello is this Youtube? I've got 75,000 views on my video – 'Irish dad watches last 3 minutes of Longford-Cavan'… where do I pick up my cheque?"

Act Nothing Like How You Act At Home – just because you haven't cleaned your oven in 3 years doesn't mean you leave a mess around for the locals in Bordeaux to pick up. At home, some feel the main streets of the nation are purely for practicing chewing gum drop-kicks, but on tour, you simply must clean up after yourselves (this works best when clumsily edited alongside some footage of rioting Russian fans, but it's a winner all by itself really). And if you find it difficult to record yourself and clean up the mean streets of Bordeaux at the same time… don't worry, there's always point no.1. "IRISH FANS OUT-DO THEMSELVES… GOD WE'RE ALL SUCH LEGENDS"

When Iceland stunned the world in June with their 2–1 win over England at the Euros, we welcomed Icelandic writer and historian Anton Ingi Sveinbjörnsson to our Irish Times podcast to explain what the night was like for his country. You loved him, we did too, so we've invited him back to give his account of one of the highlights of 2016.

Little old Iceland beat mighty England. The richest football association in the world, a country of 53 million people and "the home of football" defeated by an island in the North-Atlantic that, up until a few years ago, could only play football for 5 months of the year. To put into context how tiny this country is, in the event of a catastrophic natural disaster you could house 27% of the Icelandic population in Wembley stadium. As Gary Lineker stated in utter disbelief after the final whistle, we are a country "that has more volcanoes than professional footballers."

For us Icelanders we felt as big as we've ever felt. As a small nation we're very proud of what we achieve on the international stage. We often compare ourselves

THE VIKING

19.0208° W

INVASION

BY ANTON INGI SVEINBJÖRNSSON

to the rest of the world using the per capita metric. It makes us feel really good about ourselves, and everyone in Iceland knows what we have achieved per capita. For example, everyone here learns that we have the most Nobel-prize winners per capita of any nation in the world [Spoiler: It's 1]. If you tweaked enough variables and applied the right metrics, you could make a case to say Iceland is the best at everything.

So what a surreal feeling it was to actually have the eyes of the world on us for an international achievement that stands up

beyond our per capita metric, an achievement that spawned a whole new level of intrigue in my country. For the first time ever, questions advanced beyond "Do you guys live in snow houses?", "Do you know Björk?", and "Do Sigur Rós lyrics mean anything or do they just make up words?"

Our journey at the Euros was about that wonderfully pure emotion that only sport can bring. It's about channelling your inner child and the feeling that made you fall in love with the game. It's the indivisible bond that you share with a perfect stranger just because they happened to be next to you when THAT moment happened. It's the unerring belief

you get that anything is possible.

Growing up in Iceland to a team that was never even involved in major competitions was strange. We idolised our boys but could never properly root for them. Everyone in Iceland had another side they supported during tournaments - that was the extent of our ambition. The biggest occasions in international football were when a bigger team came to play us at home. People flocked in to see them play. To every generation of Icelander, the peak of international football was when you got a chance to

see some of the best players in the world, marvel at them, ask for autographs... and hope they didn't beat us too badly. Growing up, that all made perfect sense, that was the way things had always been and would always be. Euro 2016 changed all that.

Every one of these players feels relatable to us and, given Iceland's limited gene pool, most of them are actually related to us. These are just guys I played against as a kid. They went to school with my friends or family. This team are made up of the guys who, just like me, grew up at a time when a draw in the qualifiers in 1998 was the biggest thing we had ever accomplished. Now the kids in the

playgrounds back home can't pick teams because everyone wants to be Iceland and no one wants to be on the side playing against Iceland. To us, that is the true beauty of it. This is what the game of football is all about.

Of course this change hasn't happened overnight. This was not a freak accident. This is the result of investment in coaching and an investment in the players that we have. But a key difference, and one which I think separates Iceland from most other countries, is that the investment and the infrastructure and the coaching still haven't taken away from the fact that sometimes sport is just

> **TO EVERY GENERATION OF ICELANDER, THE PEAK OF INTERNATIONAL FOOTBALL WAS WHEN YOU GOT A CHANCE TO SEE SOME OF THE BEST PLAYERS IN THE WORLD, MARVEL AT THEM, ASK FOR AUTOGRAPHS... AND HOPE THEY DIDN'T BEAT US TOO BADLY.**

for the sake of sport. We have built football pitches at every school in the country, but the objective isn't just to produce professional players. Anyone can play, whether for love of the game, because all their friends do or just if there's nothing else to do. Kids can play football when they want, where they want. They can do so regardless of socio-economic status, age or background.

The Icelandic set up is in stark contrast with, fittingly enough, England's. Though they are the richest football association in the world, everything is set up in a system of sink or swim, and with an overemphasis on results. The need for instant impact and immediate results produces some of the world's best teenagers (Michael Owen/ Wayne Rooney), but they discard the late bloomers. With England there is no Miroslav Klose or Didier Drogba who start playing professionally at 22 and change the game. Jamie Vardy is the exception, and a new one at that. Iceland has given kids the freedom to develop, to grow, to make mistakes, to just keep it fun. It's not all about the end product.

The miracle of Iceland however is not the overcoming of odds or the coming together of plans and initiatives. It's not about the virtues of coaching, the importance of infrastructure or the value of teamwork. It isn't even about results or playing in a major tournament. It's something simpler, something much more powerful. The true Icelandic miracle is seeing little kids now so excited about seeing their country play. It's about fans filling the stadium to see OUR players and doing so with the same enthusiasm, regardless of the opposition. For the first time in my life I hear people talk about their hopes for future competitions. At a time when astronomical amounts of money separate footballers from the people who love them, Iceland at the Euros offered something special.

Anyone who has grown up seeing their country play at the highest level will never be able to grasp how much this means to us. This feeling of recognition and respect means everything. We have finally arrived on the big stage. This is where we belong.

What we have accomplished will last for a lifetime, and beyond. Generations to come will be bored to death of the story of Euro 2016. I can tell my grandkids that I kept a clean sheet against Kolbeinn Sigþórsson, something neither England nor France can claim to have done. Because that's just the kind of story this is. This team is ours.

JOE HART! JOEEEEEEE HAAAAAAART!!
HOW THE WINNER HAPPENED WITH ANALYSIS FROM KEN EARLY

1. DANNY ROSE COMES OUT TO PRESS GUDMUNDSSON, WITH RAHEEM STERLING COVERING AT LEFT-BACK. ROONEY, ENGLAND'S CAPTAIN, STANDS GUARD - NOT IN SUCH A POSITION AS TO ACTUALLY BLOCK A PASS TO ICELAND'S MOST CREATIVE PLAYER, GYLFI SIGURDSSON, BUT CLOSE ENOUGH TO THE DEFENCE TO SHOW HOW MUCH HE CARES.

2. ENGLAND'S DEFENSIVE MIDFIELDER ERIC DIER FIXES THE BALL WITH A LASER-LIKE GAZE. YOU CAN'T FOOL HIM. HE KNOWS EXACTLY WHERE THAT BALL IS...RIGHT?

3. GUDMUNDSSON IS UNDER PRESSURE FROM ROSE AND HIS PASS INSIDE TO SIGURDSSON ISN'T AS CRISP AS HE'D LIKE. BUT ROONEY'S NOT IN A POSITION TO BLOCK IT, AND ... OOOPS! ERIC DIER HAS JUST NOTICED THAT GYLFI SIGURDSSON IS BEHIND HIM!

4. DIER AND ALLI CLOSE SIGURDSSON DOWN BUT HE'S ALREADY PLAYED IT FIRST TIME TO BODVARSSON. NOW ICELAND HAVE A TWO-ON-TWO AGAINST ENGLAND'S CENTRAL DEFENDERS, GARY CAHILL AND CHRIS SMALLING.

5. THEY ARE A PARTNERSHIP OF FIRE AND ICE. ONE LIKES TO DIVE HEAD FIRST INTO PROBLEMS. THE OTHER LIKES TO THINK BEFORE HE ACTS. CAHILL GLANCES TOWARD SIGÞÓRSSON. SMALLING HAS BODVARSSON IN HIS SIGHTS. BODVARSSON TAKES A TOUCH.

6. SMALLING STANDS WITH HIS LEGS APART, BENDS SLIGHTLY AT THE WAIST, AND STARES AT THE ICELANDIC PLAYER, AS THOUGH SIZING UP A PUTT AT THE MASTERS. CAHILL ABANDONS SIGÞÓRSSON AND BOUNDS TOWARDS BODVARSSON LIKE A POLICE DOG. BODVARSSON PASSES TO SIGÞÓRSSON

7. CAHILL SLAMS THE BRAKES AND U-TURNS TOWARDS SIGÞÓRSSON. THE IMPERTURBABLE SMALLING WATCHES WITH INSCRUTABLE CALM. SIGÞÓRSSON TOUCHES THE BALL RIGHT, WRONG-FOOTING CAHILL, WHO SLAMS ON THE BRAKES AGAIN AND DOES ANOTHER U-TURN.

8. SMALLING OBSERVES THE UNFOLDING SITUATION WITH LOFTY DETACHMENT. SIGÞÓRSSON IS NOW IN ENGLAND'S PENALTY AREA BUT HE STILL HAS TIME TO TAKE ANOTHER TOUCH. JOE HART BOUNCES ON THE BALLS OF HIS BANANA BOOTS, READY FOR ACTION.

9. SIGÞÓRSSON HITS A LOW SHOT. JOE HART DIVES SLOWLY TO HIS LEFT AND GETS A HAND TO THE BALL AS IT PASSES HIM BY. HE TAKES JUST ENOUGH PACE OFF THE SHOT THAT HE IS ABLE TO TURN HIS HEAD AND ACTUALLY WATCH THE BALL ROLL INTO THE BACK OF THE NET.

10. CAHILL SCREAMS AND WAVES HIS ARMS SO HARD IT'S LIKE HE'S TRYING TO SHAKE THEM OFF HIS BODY.

THE END...

KILLING THE VIKING THUNDERCLAP

Remember thinking 'what the hell is that?!' when you first heard the "HUH" in the middle of Iceland's football matches at the Euros? What a haunting, original, powerful spectacle; this was a country different to the rest, proudly expressing its togetherness and individuality at the same time. We looked with amazement at the footage of captain Aron Gunnarsson leading the chant haka-like in front of the adoring fans in that one corner of the Allianz Riviera in Nice. A week later, the team's homecoming in Reykjavik saw one third of the entire country gather in one place to once again proudly show off their thunderclap in footage the whole world saw. We ate it up. Anton was there and says it was a "rush that I might never experience again for the rest of my life. It was an event so powerful in the nation's spirit that it felt like a second independence day."

It didn't take long for it to become REALLY annoying, did it? From that point on we have witnessed the Thunderclap being destroyed thousands of times at a variety of events around the world, and we're not just talking sport. Wolves draw 2-2 with Rotherham in an early season Championship game? Post-match thunderclap. Tipp homecoming? Thunderclap. The O'Donovan brothers return to Skibbereen? Cue a shocker of a thunderclap (a completely out of sync attempt with the crowd clapping and slapping at a whole host of incorrect moments which was of course described as 'brilliant' and 'haunting' by the Irish media). Galway bid to be the 2020 European Capital of Culture? Terrible thunderclap. Rose of Tralee escorts promoting the event before the night itself? A fucking thunderclap.

We beg you, no more.

Cut out and keep this anti-thunderclap badge! Wear with pride and point directly to it when asked to thunderclap at inappropriate times.

VIKING THUNDER FACTS

1. On the night of the Iceland v England match, 150,000 Icelandic viewers tuned in to watch their team's historic win. It was discovered that only 298 viewers were watching all the other channels in Iceland combined.

2. The odds of every child born in Iceland going on to represent the national team is 2000-1.

3. Iceland were 250-1 to qualify for Euro 2016.

4. If Russia took the same number of players per capita as Iceland did, they would have had a squad of 11,000 men at Euro 2016.

5. Since Lars Lagerbäck took over as Iceland manager, they have risen more than 100 places in the official FIFA rankings.

6. There are only 21,500 registered football players in all of Iceland.

DANNY BAKER
RAGE-O-METER

The greatest thing to come from Iceland's magical victory over England was not the unification of a nation, or a break from the commercial and financial dominance of sport. It wasn't even Chris Waddle calling all the England players 'headphones'. It was the series of tweets Danny Baker (@Prodnose) released in the immediate aftermath of the match. In just over an hour, from 9.50pm (at full-time) to 11.01pm, Baker tweeted 17 times and over the next 72 hours gained over 11,000 new followers. We now present to you the Danny Baker Rage-O-Meter where we rate our favourite tweets from those epic 71 minutes. Here's the top 5...

5.

Danny Baker @prodnose · Following

Absolutely disgraceful, #England. You useless over paid, over indulged mollycoddled shits. You are beyond shame. Disgrace to working people.

RETWEETS 4,091   LIKES 5,253

"Mollycoddled Shits" – 9.50pm
Danny's first tweet of the series was cutting but somewhat restrained with no use thus far of particularly bad language - 'mollycoddled shits' aside. Baker cleverly gets twitter's vast working class on board with his reference to 'working people'.

4.

Danny Baker @prodnose · Following

You fucking disgrace. You fucking disgrace. England footballers each and every one of you and your fucking manager are a fucking disgrace.

RETWEETS 3,453   LIKES 3,889

"Fucking Disgrace" – 9.52pm
Two minutes later Danny calls all the England players and their 'fucking manager' a 'fucking disgrace' three times in 140 characters. Impressive in itself.

3.

Danny Baker @prodnose · Following

You fucking awful craven humiliating disgrace. Go on you fuckers pick up your PL wages you cheap shits. You worms. Fuck you.

RETWEETS 2,215   LIKES 2,693

'Worms' Part 1 – 9.54pm
The first appearance of the fantastic term 'worms' that Bakers displayed a fondness for. Extra marks for the final 'Fuck you' that was somewhat unnecessarily added but drove home the point.

2.

Danny Baker @prodnose · Following

Nobody NOBODY should buy a single ticket to these empty fuckers World 'Cup qualifiers. Why? They are a piss taking disgrace. Fuck England.

RETWEETS 1,340   LIKES 1,729

Empty Fuckers – 9.59pm
There's something about 'empty fuckers' that is particularly derogatory. Plus this tweet contains the first time he actually abuses his whole country with 'Fuck England'.

1.

Danny Baker @prodnose · Following

All you mob who turned out for England tonight are a laughing stock. A low point in the game. Ridiculous clowns. Fuck off you worms.

RETWEETS 468   LIKES 710

Worms Part 2 – 10.11pm
'Worms' returns but this time he refers to ALL of the England fans who were in the stadium supporting their team. Yes, not just the players but ALL of the supporters who travelled to Nice were "ridiculous clowns." Takes a fair bit of rage (and wine) to take on a nation, well played Danny.

1930: Iceland's first international match. A sweet victory away to the Faroe Islands, 0-1.

1946: Iceland's first match officially recognised by FIFA v Denmark. Lost 0-3 at home.

1947: First international victory against Finland.

1954: Iceland's application to take part in the qualification stages of the 1956 European Championship is rejected.

1957: Iceland come last in their qualification group for the 1958 World Cup.

1998: Drew 1-1 at home to world champions France in Euro 2000 qualifying campaign.

2003: Iceland had its best ever performance in a qualifying tournament, finishing third, 1 point behind Scotland.

2013: Almost qualify for a FIFA World Cup. Played Croatia in a two-leg qualification playoff but lost 2-0 on aggregate.

2015: Qualify for Euro 2016 after beating Holland home and away in qualification and finishing second in group A.

2016: Reach quarter-finals of Euro 2016.

DROIT AU BUT

Ken Early:
THE MARSEILLE YEARS
Part Deux

After unexpectedly low sales last Christmas for his autobiography, Ken has allowed us to publish three more extracts from *Early To Bed, Early Surprise*. In these three myth-busting, post-football chapters, Ken talks about his love affair with rural Bulgaria, his tempestuous first marriage to a French sex symbol, and the phone call that saved his life... and if you like what you see, keep an eye out for *Early To Bed, Early Surprise*, available in all good bargain bins now!!! (beside *Second Captains Sports Annual, Volume 1*)

Extrait Numéro Un – Palme D'or To Europop

Having said goodbye to football, my future was unclear. I had numerous offers in the fashion business, and there was certainly much to recommend me in that world, given my hard-earned reputation as the most devastating clothes-horse south of Bordeaux.

But I had fallen in with a group of avant-garde videographers whose work piqued my interest. They had an idea – they would film me watching every minute of every game I had played in professional football in a disused cinema in one of the banlieues of Marseille, and release it as a documentary. The results were stunning. It won the Palme d'Or at Cannes (beating out stiff competition from *Stop! Or My Mom Will Shoot*, and *Honey I Blew Up The Kid*), and to the

outside world it seemed that I was set fair for a seamless transition into the world of film.

But behind the scenes, trouble was brewing. The editing process had been tortuous. I believed that for a truly honest portrayal of my experience, they should release all the footage, as a 214-hour piece of cinema *verité*. But, eager to turn a quick buck, they went for the multiplex-friendly running time of 7 hours, 43 minutes, which I felt was a disgusting misrepresentation of my 'in-the-moment', visceral responses. I vowed to leave behind the sick, money-fuelled, rat-race that is the silent documentary movie business... and enter the world of pop.

I had a number of good contacts in the music business, having partied with

Elton John and Phil Collins extensively throughout my time at Marseille (I actually appear briefly in the video for *Another Day in Paradise,* from the *...But Seriously* album by Phil, or Mr Collins as I would affectionately call him).

I had a couple of great years touring my unique brand of Euro-Pop with such luminaries as EMF, Enigma and Haddaway. Even now, when I go to remote rural parts of Bulgaria, it's impossible for me to walk down the street without someone shouting lyrics at me from *Let Me Live In Your Panties,* my 1994 club classic.

Extrait Numéro Deux – The comeback

From Stettin in the Baltic to Trieste in the Adriatic, an Iron Curtain of pop had descended on Eastern Europe, and I was holding the pull-cord. It was 1995, and on the surface, my life appeared to be perfect. But something was missing. I still yearned for football. I had no intention of leaving the city of Marseille, but my first love had cut me loose (see chapter 12: *'The fans, players and owners of FC Olympique de Marseille are a pack of stupid pricks').*
An outlet was given to me by Colonel Muammar Gaddafi, the benevolent

leader of the sylvan North African paradise of Libya. I was brought in to form a partnership with Al-Saadi Gaddafi, son of the Colonel, who was an up-and-coming young golador at the time.

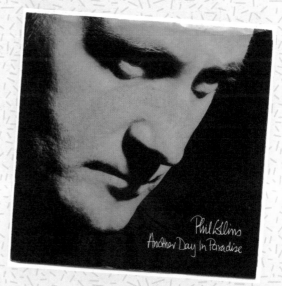

You've probably seen the Youtube clip dozens of times, but the winner we got in the Libyan Cup final of 1996 remains one of my favourite ever goals. As you'll recall, I beat three players down the right, before rabona-crossing for Al-Saadi, or Gads as I called him, to control at the back post. He expertly took the ball down, told the covering defenders what he'd do to them if they dared tackle him, before calmly slotting the ball past the goalkeeper who had momentarily absented himself from the penalty area. Truly he was a man who could do things you'd never seen on a football field before. An innovator. Great memories!

I had a tremendous time with the Oppressors for a season and a half, and I would gladly have stayed longer, but there were elements in the Libyan government who were convinced my free-wheelin' European ways were culturally unfit for the country at that time.

I promised to tone down some of my more overtly-sexual goal celebrations, but soon after that they became aware of my double life as a pop star. My future in Libya was sealed the second they heard the bass drop on *Animal Tug,* the first single from my fourth studio album of the same name.

Extrait Numéro Trois – The Irish Pub

I was low after how the Libyan adventure ended, no doubt about it. I returned to Marseille and fell into a spiral of reckless draughts-playing that nearly ended my marriage to French actress and sex-kitten Romane Bohringer before it had even begun.

Once I had extricated myself from the draughts goons that ran the scene in Marseille, I threw myself with renewed gusto into a new business venture – a beautiful, classy, understated Irish bar called "Filthy McNasty's Olde-Time Irish Drink Hole." The hours were long, and my new bride grew restless. That

handsome bastard Vincent Cassel always seemed to be around, offering Romane new roles (alongside him, of course) on an almost daily basis. Romane was a dear, sweet person but I was consumed by jealousy.

Filthy's was a roaring success from the start. Darling of the Socialist left Lionel Jospin, soon to be elected Prime Minister, DJed the opening night, and it soon became the place to be for the 'In' crowd. Rather than finding the smell of stale beer and piss a turn-off, the Marseille glitterati loved its simple, Irish charms. I was making more money than a 17th-century Dutch spices trader, but I could barely look at myself in the mirror. The Aran sweater and peaked cap that I insisted on wearing behind the bar could hide neither my own self-loathing, nor extreme body odour.

I had run foolishly, headlong into marriage. I was unhappy at work. And I stank like shit. Something had to change. Marseille had gobbled me up and spat me out, like many an able seaman before me. And then came the phone-call that saved my life. "Hey Ken, its Eoin McDevitt here. Wanna come home and dream it all up again?" I kissed Romane goodbye, and headed once more for Dublin.

GO TO PAGE 97

In an Olympics that was dominated by controversy out of the sporting arena, Amy O'Connor profiles the athlete who accidentally became a worldwide headline at Rio 2016 – Ryan Lochte.

THE PANTOMIME VILLAIN

WHAT WOULD RYAN LOCHTE DO?

In late August, mere days after he was caught out in the most epic lie imaginable, it was announced that swimmer Ryan Lochte would be participating in the new season of *Dancing with the Stars*. As a career move, it made perfect sense. As both an athlete striving to remain relevant following the Olympics Games and a public figure seeking to rehabilitate his image, Lochte fit the profile of many a *Dancing with the Stars* contestant.

At the time, a source close to Lochte (read: harried publicist) told the celebrity tabloid *US Weekly*, "Doing DWTS will be great for Ryan's image! He will be able to show America that he's a good guy who made a mistake. He's still an Olympic champion! He will be great on the show."

In other words: this has to work. We have no plan B. Please God let this work.

Prior to Rio 2016, Ryan Lochte announced his intention to shed the frat boy image he had spent so many years cultivating. In an interview with *GQ* ('The De-Bro-ing of Ryan Lochte'), he disowned his popular catchphrase 'Jeah!' and exhibited a level of maturity that we had not seen in him before. "Now that I'm more mature, it's time to focus more on the swimming part and less on the outside part."

For Lochte, that outside part had threatened to overshadow the swimming part on many occasions. Despite his sterling performances across three Olympic Games, Lochte

had become known to the general public as a handsome oaf with a penchant for wearing diamond-encrusted grills and getting 'turned up'. The most-viewed Ryan Lochte videos on YouTube didn't showcase, say, his medal-winning swimming performances, but rather his cringeworthy media appearances. For instance, two videos entitled 'AWKWARD INTERVIEW: Ryan Lochte's terrible interview with Fox 29 anchors' and, simply, 'Ryan Lochte is terrible at interviews' have cumulative viewing figures of over nine million.

Yes, this was the Ryan Lochte the world knew and loved to make fun of. But a few weeks shy of his 32nd birthday, perhaps aware that he could be nearing the twilight of his elite swimming career, he was keen for the world to look beyond his bro-child antics and take him seriously as an athlete.

***

Lochte came to the world's attention in 2004 when he competed at his maiden Olympic Games in Athens. By that point, he was a distinguished collegiate swimmer with the University of Florida and had racked up innumerable honours within the NCAA (National College Athletics Association) and the SEC (South Eastern Conference). Indeed, his profile on his college swim team's website still proudly boasts of the time he won a 400m individual medley race despite his goggles breaking when he dove into the pool at the beginning of the race.

In Athens, he qualified for just one individual event, the 200m IM, a race he would later become synonymous with. Lochte progressed to the final where he

was pitted against none other than Michael Phelps. In the end, Phelps won the race, but Lochte overcame a dogfight for second place and won the silver medal. At the end of the race, Phelps could be heard saying, "1, 2, baby!" and the two baby-faced bros warmly embraced, a scene that would be repeated countless times over the next twelve years.

By the time Beijing rolled around, Lochte had won eight World Championship medals including his first individual gold. He was twice named NCAA Swimmer of the Year. He signed a lucrative ten-year deal with Speedo. In other words, everything was coming up Lochte.

> "IT MEANS ALMOST LIKE EVERYTHING, LIKE HAPPY, LIKE IF YOU HAVE A GOOD SWIM, YOU SAY, 'JEAH'. LIKE, IT'S GOOD. SO, I GUESS... IT MEANS GOOD."

At the 2008 Olympic Games, he qualified for three individual events, including the 200m backstroke, which earned him his first individual Olympic gold. His final medal haul was two golds and two bronze medals, an impressive feat even if it paled in comparison to Phelps' eight golds.

It was around this time that we were afforded our first real insight into the mind of Lochte. The swimmer regaled journalists with tales of horsing into complimentary McDonald's for breakfast, lunch and dinner during the Games. (Not unlike Usain Bolt who once claimed that he subsisted on McNuggets in Beijing.) He admitted to forgetting to tie his swimsuit before competing in the 200m backstroke final, resulting in his suit filling with water during the race.

Arguably the most quintessential Lochte incident came early on in the Games when poor Ryan fell ill with a stomach flu after he drank tap water in Beijing. This despite the fact that Team USA were specifically warned in a meeting not to ingest the tap water in China and to stick to bottled water only. He told a swimming publication at the time, "I think I slept through it, or I wasn't paying attention, because when I went there, the first thing I started using was tap water to brush my teeth." It was a classic

> ## "MY NAME IS RYAN LOCHTE AND I'M A SIX-TIME OLYMPIC GOLD MEDALLIST. BUT RECENTLY I'VE BEEN IN THE MEDIA FOR THE WRONG REASONS."

Lochte mistake made all the more embarrassing when his father went to the entertainment show *Access Hollywood* with the big scoop. Their headline? "U.S. Swimmer Ryan Lochte Is Sick With The Runs".

These incidents helped lay the blueprint for the slightly dim slacker we would all come to know, love and mock during London 2012. But while Lochte gave us a small glimpse into his persona in Beijing, he went full throttle in the build-up to London.

He began to post well-meaning, if poorly constructed, inspirational tweets. ("Always reach for the moon cuz if u slip up u will still

be a star!!") He started referring to his fans as the "Lochtenators" and "Lochte Nation". He was apparently so allergic to the idea of commitment that his own mother went on television to say that he preferred one night stands to relationships. He began sporting a not-at-all tacky $25,000 American flag grill over his teeth. And, most importantly, he tried very, very hard to make the catchphrase "Jeah!" happen.

If anything captures the essence of Ryan Lochte, it's the word jeah. (Sort of pronounced like 'chia' but with a 'j'). Jeah is an exclamation that

Lochte borrowed from the rapper Young Jeezy and tweaked a little. It means nothing and everything at the same time, as Lochte explained back in 2012. "It means almost like everything, like happy, like if you have a good swim, you say, 'Jeah'. Like, it's good. So, I guess… it means good."

Lochte began punctuating all his tweets with #jeah and it seemed that there was no major life event that didn't earn a 'jeah'. When his sister gave birth to his nephew? Jeah. When Gillette sent him a diamond-encrusted razor? Jeah. When his tan

began to fade while on holidays in France? Jeah. He was so eager to make jeah happen that he sought to trademark it and began selling #JEAH merchandise, including a pair of sunglasses that had an American flag emblazoned on one lens and 'REEZY JEAH' printed on the other.

Despite the 'outside part' threatening to overshadow the 'swimming part', Lochte managed to summon another outstanding performance in London. He won two golds, two silvers and a bronze, and in perhaps the sweetest victory of all, he managed to defeat his

long-time rival Michael Phelps in the 400m individual medley to take the gold.

Afterwards, Lochte found himself propelled to fame. His bro antics had left an indelible impression on the world and he was soon doing the rounds on late night television and having his abs groped by morning news anchors. He made a cameo on *30 Rock* as a 'sex idiot' i.e. a good-looking moron one of

CONTINUED OVER PAGE

the characters is happy to have sex with. And in a move that almost certainly overestimated Ryan Lochte's ability to create compelling drama, he became the star of his very own E! reality show.

What Would Ryan Lochte Do? aired in the spring of 2013 and made Keeping Up With The Kardashians seem like high art by comparison. The show didn't exactly have a conceit per se and mostly just followed Lochte going about his business. The premiere episode featured Lochte uttering non-sequiturs like, "1, 2, 3, jeah!" and "Let's turn it up!" We saw him go bowling with his family, blow off steam with his friends and turn up at a training session with a hangover. We witnessed him blank upon being asked how many Olympic medals he had. When asked if he was a player or a douchebag, he responded by asking the interviewer to define those words. He declared *What Women Want* to be his favourite film... and then proceeded to refer to it as *What Woman Want* for the rest of the scene. The central joke of the show was, "Wow, this guy is very dumb," but that's a gag that can only be taken so far before it begins to wear thin. Needless to say, the show was not renewed and Lochte faded into Olympian obscurity until 2016.

Which brings us to Rio.

Lochte had bid adieu to jeah and his interviews in the lead up to the Olympics focused on getting older, his legacy and, of course, his rivalry with Michael Phelps, who had pledged to retire following the Olympics. Lochte was more contemplative than before. In one interview, he was asked how he thought his career would have panned out had he not come up in the same era as the greatest of all-time. "I guess you would say I'd be like the Michael Phelps of swimming if he wasn't there," came the reply. And while it's easy to snigger at Lochte's assertion, he isn't far off.

After winning a sixth gold medal in Brazil, Lochte finished the meet with a career total of 12 Olympic medals, placing him second only to Phelps. That's in addition to 27 World Championship medals and three FINA Male Swimmer of the Year honours. It's a remarkable record that places him at the vanguard of his sport.

For once, the swimming part seemed to be eclipsing the outside part.

That is, until he told that blasted lie.

On the morning of August 15th, an Australian journalist named Ben Way happened to be on a shuttle bus when he got talking to a woman. Over the course of their conversation, the woman mentioned that her son had been mugged the night before. "Oh really? Who's your son?" he asked. "Ryan Lochte," she replied.

Subsequently, Way posted a tweet that read, "BREAKING: @USASwimming Gold medallist Ryan Lochte has been held up at gunpoint at a party in Brazil." Soon, Lochte was being cornered by NBC's Billy Bush for an impromptu beachside interview and what clearly started as a lie to his mother was spiralling out of control.

By now, you know what happened. Lochte and his cohorts claimed to be pulled over by men posing with police badges and held up at gunpoint. Soon, however, their

> **WHEN ASKED IF HE WAS A PLAYER OR A DOUCHEBAG, HE RESPONDED BY ASKING THE INTERVIEWER TO DEFINE THOSE WORDS.**

stories began to diverge and suspicious Brazilian authorities began to investigate the incident. The likes of Billy Bush were still inclined to believe Lochte because he didn't seem like the sort who could "weave a brilliant tale." But within days, their accounts had been thoroughly debunked by contradictory CCTV evidence and claims that Lochte et al had vandalised a gas station and willingly handed over money as compensation to the station owners.

Lochte couldn't have handled the situation any worse if he had tried.

Not only did he repeatedly lie or, if you're being generous, embellish the truth, but he also skipped out of town and left his much younger teammates to clean up the mess. He reinforced every unsavoury stereotype of Americans abroad. The once-lovable douchebag had used up all sympathy credits with the media and general public, and what ensued was a spectacular fall from grace.

He issued an apology via social media in which he apologised for not being more "careful and candid" in his account and assured fans that he had learned some "valuable lessons" over the course of the whole ordeal. In the meantime, he became a laughing stock. He was the butt of countless Twitter jibes. Venerable publications like *The Washington Post* proclaimed him to be 'the dumbest bell that ever rang'. Sponsors like Speedo, Ralph Lauren and Gillette fled, forcing Lochte to ink sponsorship deals for throat drops and personal alarms.
Enter *Dancing with the Stars*.

And so, on September 12th, our hero found himself decked out in a corny white suit, preparing to dance a foxtrot on *Dancing with the Stars* in a last-ditch attempt to demonstrate contrition for his actions in Rio.

"My name is Ryan Lochte and I'm

a six-time Olympic gold medallist," Lochte told the viewer at home in his pre-dance segment. "But recently I've been in the media for the wrong reasons." In a nod to the controversies that dogged him going into the competition, Lochte and his dance partner Cheryl Burke danced to *Call Me Irresponsible*. (Heh heh, get it?)

In the end, Lochte acquitted himself perfectly well and finished the night with a respectable 24 out of a possible 40. That score put him just below Vanilla Ice, but ahead of former Texas governor Rick Perry. Small victories.

But just as everything seemed to be going off without a hitch, the outside part got in the way of the dancing part. Two protesters sporting anti-Lochte t-shirts, clearly upset that the integrity of *Dancing with the Stars* was being compromised, stormed the stage and had to be subdued by security. The men later stated that they did it for America and that Lochte was a liar. The story dominated headlines the next day, the swimmer's charming foxtrot a distant memory and his comeback now in jeopardy.

And somewhere Ryan Lochte's publicist took a deep breath. Please God let this work.

On the 14th of August in Rio, Billy Bush of The Today Show on NBC was making his way to the USA house to do some shopping when he spotted Ryan Lochte on the street.

Rumours had just started circulating about the 'gunpoint' incident and although the IOC were denying it ever happened, Bush wanted to hear the truth from the man himself.

"Hey Lochte, did it happen?" shouted Bush.

"Yeah it happened." came the reply.

They chatted on the street for a while and when it was clear there wasn't enough time to organise a camera crew for an interview, they crossed to Ipanema beach and according to Bush "went new-school with the iphone and told the story".

Here's a transcript of the interview.

Bush: "So, what happened? You were held at gunpoint last night."

Lochte: "Yes."

Bush: "What happ...Who were you with? What time at night? Who pulled you over?"

Lochte: "I was with a couple of swimmers, we were coming back from our friends house, we got pulled over, in our...taxi, and these guys came out with a badge, a police badge, no lights, no nothing just a police badge. They pulled us over, ehhh, they pulled out their guns, they told the other swimmers to get down on the ground - they got down on the ground. I refused, I was like 'we didn't do anything wrong, so - I'm not getting down on the ground' and then the guy pulled out his gun, he cocked it, put it to my forehead and he said, 'Get down,' and I was like, I put my hands up, I was like 'whatever.'

'He took our money, he took my wallet and then...'"

Bush: "But he left your cellphone, he left your credentials"

Lochte: "He left my cellphone, he left my credentials..."

"GYBE-HO!"

SAILING FEVER INFECTED THE NATION WITH ANNALISE MURPHY'S OLYMPIC SILVER, SO FOR THE UNEDUCATED OUT THERE, HERE IS...

SIMON HICK'S

SAILING WORKSHOP
GYBE TALKING

As one half of north county Dublin's most renowned father-son sailing partnership (four time Rush Regatta champion*) AND mentor of Annalise Murphy, Simon is ideally placed to inform readers on how to 'get nauti'. Simon began his sailing journey on the mean seas of Skerries, starting out as a winch monkey before moving on to master anchor drops and mast climbing. Today, Simon can be seen performing his sea shanties, a capella, on the street and alleyways of Dublin city.

*source: Simon's dad

SIMON SEZ:
After Annalise's success in Rio, sailing is now officially Ireland's second most popular sport** after rugby, so you're gonna need to up your yachting game. The McGregor beard is soon to be replaced by over the shoulder chunk knit sweaters and 190 Euro deck shoes. Don't know your bowline from your clove hitch? Not to worry, after reading this you'll be an easy breezy sailor girl. So let's get straight into gybe talk by dealing with some of the main problems people will face over the coming months as they ultimately give up their land based existence and become full-time sailors.

**source: Simon's dad

PIER PRESSURE:
The first thing you have to realise is the hierarchy for those at sea is much stricter than for those on land, and given the limited number of positions available on board a ship, its even more difficult to move up the ranks. Plus, the motivation to

maintain or improve your status is all the greater because should the need for cannibalism arise (shipwrecked, food washed overboard, captain missed his elevenses) cabin boys and swabbies are first on the BBQ.

Moving up the chain of command is not just about improving your tiller work and navigation skills, it's about being seen to be captaincy material. That means wearing a captain style hat, nonchalantly glancing at your hand-held compass when in conversation, and never ever being seen socialising with a cabin boy or deck hand.

Remember, it's as much about pushing others down the ranks as it is about moving yourself up. Character assassination is a sailor's best friend. If you find yourself in the company of the captain you should drop hints, for example, about the quartermaster's increasing fondness for rum or that the boatswain's splicing on the halyards leaves a lot to be desired.

Homework: Watch Master and Commander

PORT AUTHORITY

Its only three months since you decided to become a sailor, and somehow you find yourself on a boat, at sea. The crew are a tight knit, knowledgeable, tough-to-impress group. Not to worry, there are a few simple shortcuts to help you win them over.

1- While scribbling in the captain's log, casually double check with a nearby crew member that there are indeed 3,038 fathoms in a league?
2- Shout "STARBOARD" and/or "MAST. ABEAM" in an angry manner at any passing yachts. This is sailing's equivalent of 'he's at it all day ref'.
3- Sit cross-legged in your white linen pants reading D.H Lawrence's The Mystic Blue. If the other crew members fail to notice, don't be afraid to read out loud.
4- Point at the clouds and say 'that's a nasty looking cumulonimbus, maybe we should batten down the hatches'.

Homework: Voyage to the Bottom of the Sea

MUTINY

Mutinies start with a careless whisper that quickly spreads like a bush fire through the have-nots. Before you know it, you're walking the plank with a cutlass between the shoulder blades. Prevention is better than cure folks, so don't be afraid to act on your paranoid delusions about those plotting

against you. Solitary confinement, extra night shifts and cutting of rations keeps the crew on edge, and leaves less time for idle gossip. Starting rumours of your own about a Jonah on board will keep the ball in your court. If the worst comes to the worst and the mutiny is already underway, immediately set your course for one of the more hospitable South Pacific islands.

Homework: Mutiny on the Bounty

SAILOR MOUTH

The key to being accepted by the ruling classes is to talk a good game, and the key to talking a good game is using non-stop sailing jargon. First of all, you want to distance yourself from the non-sailing community by referring to them as 'landlubbers'. This phrase will always get a laugh from the gang in the club bar, further cementing your association with the sea dogs. Pepper business meetings with the terms 'aft' and 'abaft'. Tell the club commodore that you love his schooner rig. Refer to ropes as sheets, alcohol as grog, the front of things as the bow, big people as ballast, call your kitchen a galley, and if anything remotely good happens in your life exclaim Huzzah!

Homework: Wind starring Matthew Modine

SHIPTEASE

The great thing about the yachty look is its predictability, its reliability and that its flattering on all figures. Invest now and you won't have to change your look for several decades. For inspiration think of Jean Paul Gaultier perfume ads, the Sinbad movies, and paintings of Lord Nelson. White circular hat tipped to one side, navy and blue striped t-shirt, bare feet, powder blue chinos rolled to mid calf, floppy hair, and depending on your social circles, a giant back tattoo of a topless mermaid. Accessorise with eye-patch, gold hooped earrings, rolled up navigation charts, an almanac under your arm, and, it goes without saying, a sextant, octant and quadrant.

Homework: Dead Calm starring Billy Zane

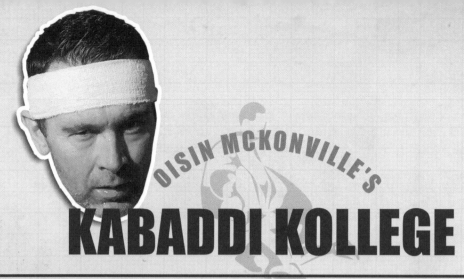

OISIN MCKONVILLE'S
KABADDI KOLLEGE

WITH ARMAGH ALL-IRELAND WINNER AND IRELAND'S KABADDI KING OISÍN MCCONVILLE

What a year for Kabaddi 2016 was. If Jaipur Pink Panthers thought they could roll up to the Gachibowli Indoor Stadium in Hyderabad this year and knock Patna Pirates off their perch as Pro Kabaddi League champions, boy did they have another thing coming.

You surely don't need reminding that Pardeep Narwal inspired the Pirates to a thrilling 37-29 victory, ensuring Arjun Singh's men became the first back-to-back winners of the title.

Ireland has since been gripped by Kabaddi fever, with boys and girls around the land dreaming of becoming the next Rahul Chaudhari or "Kabaddi Queen" Mamatha Poojary. But do these kids fully understand the skills required to master this ancient Indian game?

Oisin McConville certainly does

and as Ireland's foremost outdoor Kabaddi enthusiast, he's here to help. Welcome to McKonville's Kabaddi Kollege...

Oisin says *"HI I'M OISIN MCCONVILLE. CROSSMAGLEN HAS LONG BEEN KNOWN AS THE KABADDI CAPITAL OF IRELAND. THE SKILLS I'M ABOUT TO IMPART WERE LEARNED ON THE MAIN SQUARE IN THE TOWN AND TRANSFERRED TO THE GAA FIELD, HELPING CROSSMAGLEN RANGERS WIN OUR 6 ALL-IRELAND CLUB TITLES."*

SKILL 1 - THE RAID:
This is the bread and butter of Kabaddi, the ability of one man to raid the opponents' half of the court, pick off as many of the seven defenders as he can and make it back to the safety of his own half without being tackled. Moves employed to tag the defenders can include the reverse kick and the foot touch, which Oisin expertly demonstrates with scant regard for his own personal safety.

SKILL 2 –
WEAR APPROPRIATE CLOTHING:
Topless. Knees bandaged. Barefoot. This may not seem like a skill but by wearing enough bandaging, the great Kabaddi players confuse their opponents into thinking they have more injuries than they have. This tactic can be transferred to the GAA field or in life in general; Crossmaglen won a minor title in 1994 completely in Kabaddi attire and the people of Crossmaglen often dressed as Kabaddi players to confuse British army helicopters during the same period.

3.

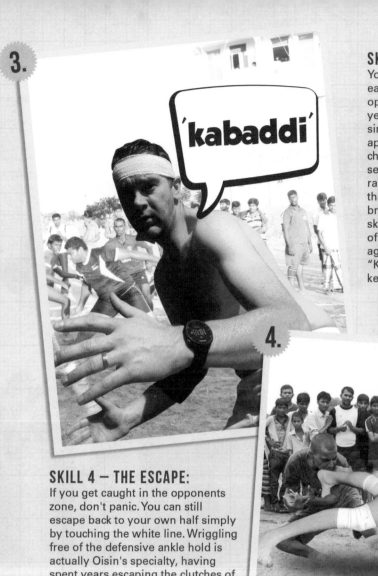

SKILL 3 - THE CANT:

You thought Skill 1 sounded easy easy enough? Well try raiding the opponents' half while repeatedly yelling the word "Kabaddi" in a single breath. Known as the approved cant of the sport, the chanting of this word for up to 30 seconds shows the referee that the raider is constantly exhaling rather than inhaling or simply holding his breath. Again Oisin has used this skill to confuse on the GAA grounds of Ireland, famously scoring his goal against Kerry in 2002 whilst roaring "Kabaddi" in the face of Kingdom keeper Declan O'Keefe.

4.

SKILL 4 — THE ESCAPE:

If you get caught in the opponents zone, don't panic. You can still escape back to your own half simply by touching the white line. Wriggling free of the defensive ankle hold is actually Oisin's specialty, having spent years escaping the clutches of Francie Bellew for the sanctity of the dressing room during Armagh training sessions.

5.

OISIN SAYS -

"Traditionally, I have found it difficult to find anyone to play Kabaddi with. Don't worry if you can't gather two crews of seven, one idiot who'll play along is enough (see image). And please use the skills you have learned today with caution."

WHAT RICHARD DID

For 30 years Richard Dunne's life revolved around football. Now that he's walked away from the game, he's never been happier. He sits down with Ken to talk about the long road from Killinarden to Monaco...

The first time I met Richard Dunne face to face was the night Ireland were knocked out of the 2002 World Cup by Spain. A friend who was working with the FIFA ticketing office had heard the players were having a party in some Irish bar in Seoul. I arrived in this crowded basement bar to find the air thick with smoke and booze, got a drink and sat down at a nearby seat that was free, only to realise that the person sitting to my left with a table full of pints in front of him was Richard Dunne.

Whoever Dunne had been talking to seemed to have just gone to the bar and he was sitting there looking contented. I seized my opportunity. "Richard how are you doing?" Then I realised that I was too starstruck to think of anything interesting to say. So I started babbling, mainly in the form of a series of lame football-related questions. Before long, Dunne's

contentment had given way to mild but unmistakeable irritation. I could see him taking little glances around wondering where his mate from before had got to. I think it was the question "So... would you say Mick McCarthy is a bit like Keegan?" that eventually prompted him to say, "Emmm.. can we just not talk about football?"

During the silence that followed I nervously lit a cigarette and was surprised when Dunne asked if he could have one. Sure, I said, trying to conceal my astonishment that an international footballer would smoke. Moments later Mark Kinsella came down to the table and asked for a cigarette. He sat there smoking it cupped in his hand, taking little furtive glances around the room to see if anyone had noticed. This was quite different from Dunne, who looked quite self-assured as he puffed away. The two footballers started

talking about footballer stuff, and realising I had nothing of interest to contribute, I sidled away.

My failure to befriend Ireland's promising young defender aside, it was a good night. The place was thronged with fans but the players actually seemed to be having fun. They were swapping shirts with the fans. There was karaoke which was being led by Robbie Keane and a shirtless Gary Kelly, who was wearing a black bra, presumably thanks to one of these swaps.

I remember Alan Kelly took a liking to my t-shirt, which I had got in Tokyo the week before. It was white with a green geometric design and the word "PRIORITY" in block capitals and seemed vaguely environmental. He went to whip off his Ireland polo shirt and offered to swap. I stared at his beer- and sweat-soaked shirt... and said no. Even at the time I felt

like a bit of a dick for doing that, but it was sweaty enough in Seoul without having to wear somebody else's sweat.

I didn't realise it at the time, but that was probably the last big players-and-fans piss-up in the history of Irish football. Within a few months Ireland were booed off at Lansdowne Road for losing to Switzerland without Roy Keane, the Genesis report came out, drinking became controversial in a way it hadn't been before, relations on all sides deteriorated, things were never really the same.

Fourteen years later in a hotel bar in Dublin, I ask Dunne if he remembers that night. It seemed to me that except for the players who had missed penalties, everyone was having a great time, which some people might think was strange since the team had just been knocked out of the World Cup in sickening fashion.

"Yeah - it was a good night. It was a good squad. OK, we were disappointed that we lost. But everyone was so happy that we were going home. We'd been away for so long, it was like, yes! And we didn't go out in disgrace or anything, we'd played well. We were just unlucky…"

At the time there were a lot of people saying that Ireland hadn't been unlucky. We'd played great football in qualifying, and then our manager and best player had fallen out. We'd wasted our best chance of really doing something.

But when you spend a bit of time with Dunne you get a sense that his attitude to football and to life is more fatalistic than that. Shit happens, you've just got to deal with it.

"I didn't get involved with what was happening with Roy. The senior players were handling it. I was pissed off - I wanted him to play because he was so good. You talk about Ireland playing

good football in those years. That's because it's the only time we've had the best midfielder in the world controlling games for us. We've had great strikers, good defenders - but having that one dominant central midfielder, one who can control and dominate games, we've always struggled to find that. And Roy could do it."

"So it was disappointing at the time that he left because he was a major part of the team, a major part of getting us there. But then, we lost to Spain on penalties. I don't know if we could have done any better with him. I don't know whether he would have changed it. What more can you do?"

> "I DIDN'T REALISE IT AT THE TIME, BUT THAT WAS PROBABLY THE LAST BIG PLAYERS-AND-FANS PISS-UP IN THE HISTORY OF IRISH FOOTBALL… DRINKING BECAME CONTROVERSIAL IN A WAY IT HADN'T BEEN BEFORE, RELATIONS ON ALL SIDES DETERIORATED, THINGS WERE NEVER REALLY THE SAME."

****

When I met Dunne it was a week to the day since Robbie Keane's last game for Ireland, when 30,000 people came to watch Keane's international career receive a full state funeral. Dunne's last game for Ireland happened three years ago, a 3-1 win over Kazakhstan in a dead-rubber World Cup qualifier. Nobody knew at the time that it was going to be his last game.

His retirement from club football was equally low key. At the time even he didn't realise it had happened.

At the end of the 2014-15 season Dunne was released by QPR. He and his wife Helen went to the south of France with their two children, Tayo (10) and Lyla (7). They had been going on holidays there for nearly ten years, initially on the recommendation of his City team-mate Antoine Sibierski.

"We said let's put the kids into school for a couple of weeks. Then we can have a little holiday on our own, a bit of freedom during the day. It's a Montessori school - once you pay, you get in…So we said let's give it a try. And the kids loved it. So we ended up staying for six weeks. And then we just said… let's stay."

He only realised that he was done with football for good when he had the chance to go back to it.

"Steve Walford rang me in October and asked if I wanted to go back and play for Bolton. And that's when I just decided… nah. It was the last thing I wanted to do. They were bottom of the league, and I just thought… I've had enough. I thought I wanted to go back. I wondered: if I had the opportunity, would I actually go back and do it? Then it came, and I thought, no. I'm finished. I'm just enjoying life the way it is now."

The way life is now is that the Dunnes own a place in Monaco and another one up the coast in Antibes. I wonder what he gets up to all day.

"I don't really know. It's mad, because I do nothing… but I do loads. If I'm in France, I go down and fiddle about on the boat, me and the kids and the dogs. Or go and play football with my friends, go for a run, go swimming… Or you've got to go and meet someone in the bank, go and get something for someone, something else is broken… I should write it down, because I don't know what I do, but I've never got a free minute to myself. I always feel like I'm doing something, whether it's dropping the kids off or picking them up. It's nice..."

One thing that doesn't feature much in Dunne's life is football.

"I think that was half the reason for moving away. If I had stayed in England, I would have been in the same environment. Having the same conversations. The

was preparing for it, recovering from it. It's... it's a pain in the arse really. I was happy to finish when I finished, because it done my head in for the last bit, being injured. And when the time came, I was happy."

"So to come away from it and not be involved in it - it's really helped me. Because now I enjoy watching football, being interested, seeing

normal football fan. Everything is black or white. And it's nice to be able to relax and just judge like that, just to say "he's shit" or "he's brilliant" or whatever.. haha."

Dunne's father won the League of Ireland with Shamrock Rovers and several of his uncles also had careers in the league, but Dunne only started playing the game at the age of seven when his dad

opportunity would have come to go and play football and I would have taken it because I was there.

"Football just consumes everything. You're thinking, everything's ruined now, because we lost, or everything's great now, because we won. After nearly twenty years of that, it just grates on you. And when you step away from it you're like... alright, this doesn't actually matter. There's a match on over there and you don't notice it. My whole life was football, you start to think that's normal. Everything I did

who's signing who and this sort of stuff - being a fan again."

He can talk to his friends about football again. This wasn't always the case when he was playing. "I had no interest in talking about it with them - they all supported Liverpool. So they'd be like, what's Liverpool doing signing him? And I'd say, I don't care. I was just consumed with what was going on at my club. Or say, I'd train with a guy, my friends'd say 'he's shit'. I'd say, 'He's not shit, he's actually... really good, he's just had a bad day." But you can't explain it to a

signed him up to play in the Home Farm mini-leagues. I wonder if he was the best player in his team straight away, or if it only became apparent a bit later.

"The best player in that Home Farm team? I wouldn't have thought so, no. We had a really good team."

Who was better than you?

"Stephen McPhail - miles better. He was brilliant. There was Barry Ferguson, a centre-forward called Andrew Cullen. We'd win matches

83

"It's mad - because they're not. They're not massively better than him. There are a few really outstanding footballers. And then there are loads of players who are pretty much the same. And often what makes the difference is just one thing. It could be a lack of pace, or not being able to jump, or not having a great first touch - and someone else in your position has that one attribute that you haven't. Then you've gone behind them. You don't get that little breakthrough. Because, whatever you're missing - if you get that breakthrough, then you've made it. You've got that start, you've got that foot in the door. So if it doesn't work out at that club, some other club will take a chance, they'll say well he's played first team football. And you get the chance to develop your ability. But if you don't get the chance, you're screwed. If injuries don't come along, people don't get chances. Look at Marcus Rashford at Man United. He was nowhere. Someone got injured, and now all of a sudden he's the saviour of English football. That's it. There's a fine line between making it and not making it."

Fatalism: you can be as talented as you like, but nine times out of ten injuries decide the winners and losers.

Dunne's uncle relented when Nottingham Forest brought him and several team-mates over for a trial and asked him to sign. "I remember then me dad said: Listen. You're going to Everton." Dunne wanted to join Forest with his friends. "But that was it. It was "You're going to Everton." And I said, "right." I was a Liverpool fan. So I ruined that straightaway."

Dunne was 16 when he signed his first contract. "I remember my friends were having chats about what subjects they're gonna select in fifth year, what they're going to do next. I was like, I'm probably gonna go to England and play football. And they're like, yeah,

five and six nil, Andrew would score four or five. It didn't seem like what I was doing at the back was that important. We were a really, really good side - I think we came third in a European championships over in Belgium at U12. All the lads were getting sent away on trials, and I was never, ever sent away anywhere. My uncle at the time was a scout for Everton. And he purposely wouldn't send me away, because he thought it was favouritism."

I wonder what he thinks makes the difference between a good player and a bad player at that age. I was in school with Barry Quinn, who played alongside Dunne in the Ireland under-18 side that won the European Championships in 1998. In the opinion of Brian Kerr, he was one of the best players in that side. I knew that as a kid he was ridiculously good. I could have played football all day, every day, and never been as good as him. Can football ability really all be about practice?

"There's obviously a natural talent involved as well. You can see it in really young kids. With some of them you just know, you can do all you want for the rest of your life - but you'll never ever be a footballer. And some kids you can see they've got the natural style of how to do it."

Quinn went on to have a respectable career, winning four Ireland caps and playing his club football mainly for Coventry City and Oxford United. I tell Dunne that I remember being on a bus to a game with an English journalist who happened to be a Coventry fan. I asked what he thought of Quinn, who then would have been about 22. "Very ordinary."

I was astonished, and also a little bit crushed. I knew Quinn was absolutely brilliant. If he's "ordinary", then how good must the ones be who make it to the top?

good one."

His first couple of seasons at Everton were another lesson in how your success or failure is decided by the things you can't control. He was in the first team within 18 months, and soon enough he was back in the reserves, and it was all down to who was picking the team.

> "BUT YOU CAN'T CHANGE SOMEONE'S MIND IF THEY'RE NOT WILLING TO GIVE YOU A CHANCE. AS A PERSON IT MAKES YOU STRONGER. YOU KNOW HOW TO DEAL WITH THE SHIT, PEOPLE WHO TREAT YOU LIKE SHIT. IT WAS HORRIBLE, BUT IT'S A LIFE LESSON: THINGS AREN'T GONNA BE ROSY ALL THE WAY THROUGH."

"Dave Watson had been doing his coaching badges. He was taking a big interest in me, helping me, encouraging me. He taught me a lot of important, basic defending. You're running down the line, he'd say, you can't tackle with this leg, that's why you're taking the yellow card, you're doing it with the wrong foot. Or - if he's going for the ball, why are you stood in this position? Why don't you give yourself a better chance by dropping off five yards?

"It was really basic stuff, but if you're not taught it, well... You might figure it out for yourself. You might figure it out in a match, but you'll concede a lot of goals first. So then Joe Royle was sacked. Dave Watson became the manager and put me in for the last four or five games. So I went away for the summer happy, came back, and I only played one game the next season!"

Howard Kendall had taken over as the new permanent manager, and he didn't fancy Dunne.

"This is what happens all the way through your career. New managers come and they either like you or don't like you. There's no point in even worrying about it. Your face doesn't fit."

"I had a contract, so I knew it was alright. But it's difficult when you're 18 or 19 to grasp how this is gonna work out. You're just living it, and thinking every day - fuck, I should be doing better. But you can't change someone's mind if they're not willing to give you a chance. As a person it makes you stronger. You know how to deal with the shit, people who treat you like shit. It was horrible, but it's a life lesson: things aren't gonna be rosy all the way through. He got sacked at the end of the year, so you feel like you have a fresh chance."

The new manager was Walter Smith. The first thing he did was make a rule that the players had to come to training every morning dressed smartly in shirt and trousers. "We just used to leg it in in the tracksuit. It was a bit odd at first, but it teaches you you can't just wake up five minutes before and come in and expect to get away with things. It's for yourself, look after yourself, make yourself presentable before you do anything."

But Dunne was a young guy living alone in a different country. He was enjoying his independence a bit too much for Smith's liking. Eventually there was a big blow-up over the mega New Year's Eve of the Millennium, when Dunne and the midfielder Michael Ball

went too far.

"What happened was, I just never woke up for training. Was training at 10am? Fuck knows. I think it might have been one o'clock. We'd gone out - maybe we hadn't even gone out, maybe we had a party in my house... but there was no match for a few days anyway. We had a few drinks. I didn't wake up until the afternoon. Nobody had called me, nobody had done anything, so I was like... I think I might have got away with it. Maybe nobody noticed. And then I went down to the shop, and I saw David Unsworth. And he was like, 'Ohhh, youse two are fucked.' And I said, 'What do you mean us two?' And he was like, 'Bally didn't come in either.' And I was just..... YESSSS! I hadn't spoken to Bally or anything, but I was just like, YESSSS. I knew someone else was in it with me then, so I didn't feel as bad."

Dunne was fined two weeks wages and busted back down to the

reserves. There was more trouble the following season, when they were caught by the management giggling on the bus on the way back from a League Cup defeat at Bristol Rovers.

"It was Archie Knox actually who came down the bus. 'What the fuck are you two laughing at?' We were all chatting. We can't just sit there crying the whole way because we lost a match. Somebody did something or said something and we laughed. And because we

Smith never got bad on a personal level, but the manager was now open to offers. In 2000 Dunne was sold to Manchester City, who were managed by his old Everton boss, Joe Royle. As was becoming typical for Dunne, the new start seemed to go off the rails almost immediately, as City got relegated and Royle was sacked. But then Kevin Keegan arrived, and things started to get better fast.

"The next year, in the Championship, we pissed the

But we're going to get you fit.'"

"So I was in training at half seven in the morning on my own, then training again at five o'clock on my own. I wasn't allowed in the first-team dressing room, I wasn't allowed to be around the lads - I wasn't allowed to be a footballer any more. It was just like - come in, get one member of staff in. It was right, run to that line, then that line, then that line - run. It wasn't like now, right, you need to get fitter so you need to do all this sophisticated stuff. It was just: you're an arsehole, just fucking run, run, run. For about two months it was the same thing. Even the people that would come in and make me run felt sorry for me. They were like, "I'm sorry I

> "IT'S NOT HARD BECAUSE ... MOST OF IT - GOING OUT - IT'S BULLSHIT ANYWAY. YOU GET ALL THE PEOPLE HANGING ON TO YOU, YOU START THINKING THAT YOU'RE GREAT, YOU GET SUCKED INTO IT... AND WHEN YOU STOP, YOU LOOK BACK AND THINK, I REALLY SHOULDN'T HAVE DONE THAT FOR SO LONG."

were sitting facing up the bus, they can see us. So it's like, right, youse two. And then the whole bus was laughing, but we were the youngest two so we were easy to pick on. It makes it worse when you get caught because you just start sniggering and laughing... it was nothing to do with the match. It didn't mean we didn't care. It just meant that something funny's happened."

Dunne insists the relationship with

league. But I still wasn't behaving proper. I was drinking at the wrong time..."

What is "the wrong time"?

"Like, the night before training. There was one time I came to training, I wasn't in a great state. He could have just said, right, on your bike. But he gave me a chance, he said 'Right, listen, I don't know what to do with you, I don't know what to do with you.

have to do this, but this is the way it is..."

"Eventually I got back in the team. Usually what happens is, things go tits-up on the pitch, and they think, OK we need to change it, see how he's playing. I was 23 or 24 then. That was when I sort of accepted what being a professional was. I couldn't just be professional whatever days I wanted to be. It had to be a full-time thing. I couldn't go out, play a match and have a few drinks on Saturday, then a few more drinks on Sunday, then see what's happening on Monday... It was just about wising up, growing up. Stop taking the piss."

"Once you start being professional, it's not as hard as you thought. It's not hard because ... most of it - going out - it's bullshit anyway. You get all the people hanging on to you, you start thinking that you're great, you get sucked into it... and when you stop, you look back and think, I really shouldn't have done that for so long. But I was 22, 23 - a young guy, in a different country, living on my own... it took me longer to grow up than it should have, but I got there in the end. I enjoyed the first part of it as well."

While Keegan saw that Dunne had become more mature, his early disciplinary problems had already fixed his reputation in the eyes of many fans and journalists. And to some extent this was obviously all his fault.

And yet to some extent, it wasn't. A lot of it had to do with his build, which is massive for a footballer. At the age of 18 he was already being called the "Honey Monster" by fans at Everton. During his career, his playing weight was fifteen and a half stone, or 98kg. That would make him the heaviest outfield player in today's Premier League except for Everton's 100kg forward Romelu Lukaku. Unlike Lukaku, who at the age of 15 was already bench-pressing 100kg, Dunne was never one for pumping iron.

"When I did weights I put weight on. You'd do weight sessions as a team, but I never did any extra weights on my own. I was physically strong anyway, I didn't need it for strength. I didn't probably understand the benefits of it, in terms of making muscle stronger, leaner, more toned. I just thought, if these are complaining about me being overweight, I'm not doing weights, because that'll put weight on me. I'll get fined. So I'll just try to keep it as it is."

Did it hurt to hear people calling him fat?

"It was annoying. OK, I'm definitely not the streamlined, perfect athlete or whatever. But I was effective in the way that I was, the way my body was. That's me, I'm big. People would say I was fat. I wasn't fat, I was just big. I wasn't a big fat footballer running around. I was just bigger than everyone else on the pitch. I could still do whatever I had to do. People always want to label

you in some way. That was what they did with me, they stuck that one on me.

"It was hard. What had happened was, I stopped being a kid, and became a man. People were like, "Oh, look how he's turned his life around!" I hadn't really changed. You play well, and it's like - 'He looks skinny, he looks really fit, he looks great, he's such a professional, he's a model pro.' You play crap, and they go, 'He's

a mess. Look at the state of him.' And nothing's changed. I'm the same person, doing the same things."

"You obviously wish everybody writes nice things about you. When they don't, it's like... what the fuck does he know anyway? But it becomes a gang mentality. Someone writes something bad, fine, that's his opinion. But then someone reads it, he'll tell his mates, and they're all saying it. Everyone has to follow what

someone else says. The important thing is, is he playing well? If he's playing well, does it matter what he looks like? It's not about going out to try and look great. It's about being effective in the match.

"You get to a point and you think, what's the point in me worrying about what all these people are thinking or writing. What I worried about was: what's the manager thinking? And when I was fit, I always played. So I can't have

"It's good because it's voted for by the fans. Man City wasn't the Man City that it is now. Our goal each season was to stay up. We had an awful lot of defending to do at times. People could see that I was trying my nuts off for the team. I think that's what they appreciated. I had to be fit to do that. I had to be fit to play 35 games a season. It's nice, even now if I go back to Man

> WE HAD A CHANCE OF GETTING INTO EUROPE THROUGH UEFA FAIR PLAY. SO I SAID, 'LADS, THE RESULT WILL LOOK AFTER ITSELF. THE CLUB WANT US TO BE IN EUROPE, SO TRY NOT TO GET YELLOW CARDS, CERTAINLY NO RED CARDS.' AND I GOT SENT OFF AFTER FOUR MINUTES.

City, people say hello, they're nice to me, they're happy to see me. They know the effort I put in when I was there. So I am pleased with that. It was the biggest part of my career, being there."

In 2006 he was made captain. "I never shouted and screamed and roared. My attitude was, whatever happens, let's show that we care and we want to fight for the result. If teams are better than us, they're better than us. Never roll over and accept it..."

I immediately can't resist asking what happened that time City lost 8-1 to Middlesbrough at the end of the 2007-8 season.
"It was Sven's last match. We were sixth or seventh, something like that. We were missing out on Europe. We had a chance of getting into Europe through UEFA Fair Play. So I said, 'Lads, the result will look after itself. The club want us to be in Europe, so try not to get yellow cards, certainly no red cards.' And I got sent off

been that bad. Different managers kept picking me. So whatever was written about me can't all have been true. You can't constantly get in trouble, being unprofessional, and keep getting picked. Football is ruthless. If you keep making mistakes, you're out the door. I think when you make one mistake, people want you to make more all the time. And if they can't see it, they make a big deal out of little things."

The background noise never really went away, and from time to time Dunne would get the idea that maybe he ought to lose weight.

"There's loads of times you'd hear, you're overweight, you need to do this and that. You'd go on a ... not

diet, but you have to run, you have to be fitter, you have to get fitter... and then you're fitter, and you lose a bit of your physicality... you feel tired. Well, I felt tired. Because I wasn't living my natural life, I wasn't doing what I was supposed to be doing. So I felt weaker. So, alright, I can be dead skinny if you like, but I'll be shit, because I can't fucking run, I've no energy to do anything. So I'm better off being what I am, doing what I've been doing, and then I'll be happier, a better player, and that'll be it."

***

Dunne played the best football of his club career at City. He won the club Player of the Year award every year from 2005 to 2008.

after four minutes. Conceded a penalty and got sent off after four minutes. Fucking hell. And we got hammered 8-1."

"Then at the end of it, they said they're sacking the manager. Best season we've had for a long time. Played really good football, beat United home and away. We hadn't done that for years and years. And at the end of all that they're sacking the manager. The owner was the President of Thailand. He wanted to take us to Thailand and show us off. I was just fed up and I said, I'm not going. I ended up getting fined another two week's wages for that.

Dunne spoke to Spurs and Portsmouth over the summer of 2008 and was close to leaving, but the new manager, Mark Hughes, persuaded him to sign a new contract with City. Towards the end of that summer they were taken over by Sheikh Mansour, and became a superclub overnight.

"At the end I was pushed out. I mean, they'd got shitloads of money so they had their choice of whoever they wanted. I had my four player of the year awards, but then I didn't have a very good season. I picked the worst time to have a bad season. They signed Kolo Toure, they were trying to sign John Terry, Joleon Lescott, so I knew I was getting pushed out. They kept saying, no, we want you to be here, we're gonna play Lescott left-back, we want you to be here. And then they signed him, and they said to me, you have to go. I accepted it. Players move, I was fortunate I didn't have to move for such a long time."

"What annoyed me was, they said: 'we've signed all these players, and now we've got to sell you to balance the books.' Unless they're selling me for fifty million, it didn't make any sense. Don't bullshit me, you know what I mean? Just say, listen, thanks very much, see you

later. You're not gonna play. So yeah, that was kind of shit."

Dunne had just won his fourth City Player of the Year award when Garry Cook, City's then-CEO, said that the club were aiming for a higher calibre of superstar as "Richard Dunne doesn't roll off the tongue in Beijing".

"Yeah. Well, he was an arsehole. He was an idiot, really. Whatever he says is of no importance to me. I don't know him. He's a marketing man. He has no idea about football."

I say that you don't have to know anything about football to know that's an insulting thing to say.

"He's said worse things than that to other people which ended up getting him sacked. He was this big shot from Nike. Trying to talk his way into everything. Had all these big ideas. He was just a bullshitter, just a big bullshitter.

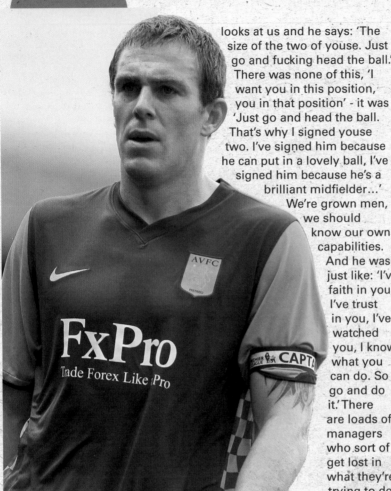

looks at us and he says: 'The size of the two of youse. Just go and fucking head the ball.' There was none of this, 'I want you in this position, you in that position' - it was 'Just go and head the ball. That's why I signed youse two. I've signed him because he can put in a lovely ball, I've signed him because he's a brilliant midfielder...' We're grown men, we should know our own capabilities. And he was just like: 'I've faith in you, I've trust in you, I've watched you, I know what you can do. So go and do it.' There are loads of managers who sort of get lost in what they're trying to do. Trying to analyse everything. With him it was simple, everyone knew their job, there was no complications."

If O'Neill's tactics were easy to understand, his thoughts were hard to read.

"He's strange in a way. If you play well, literally, you can do whatever you like, he's that happy with you. If you play bad, forget about it. He'll put the head down, walk past you in the corridor, wouldn't say anything to you. There was certain times... if someone was to make a mistake, OK they didn't play. And then, six months down the line, he'd show the video again! There was a match the season before I went, they played Hamburg. He'd given games to a few of the lads that hadn't been playing, but they lost 3-1. And he was still bringing it up when I was there the following season, still hammering people

over it. Still having a go at them! So... he has a long memory, you know what I mean?

"When he makes his mind up, it's very difficult to turn him around. That's why, in a dressing room, some people will love him and some people will hate him. Because it's either all or nothing. If you're playing, he's brilliant. You can say, listen, can I have tomorrow off? 'Yeah, absolutely! What you're doing for me is worth more than anything, you wouldn't believe it,' blah-di-blah. So the lads that are playing are like, 'brilliant, he's sound.' The ones who aren't: 'Arsehole, I don't like the way he's not speaking to me, he's not explaining to me or whatever...' What can you say to them? 'I'm alright...'"

The 2010 League Cup final with Villa was the closest Dunne came to winning a trophy in English football.

"It was weird - a big cup final, you're supposed to savour the moment and all this. We went to London on the Thursday. Stayed in the hotel, all that. Then turned up at the ground literally one hour before kick-off! There was no soaking up the atmosphere and all that stuff. It was, right, quick change and get out there and warm up. We'd been there two days before, and now you're just rushing at the last minute! But he just did things like that."

"The way he managed was like 'you might think I'm soft because I give you a day off - but never ever forget that I'm in charge.' Being the last one on the bus, making the bus wait for him, making the players wait for him - always little hints along the way: don't mess with me, I'm the boss. And it worked. It was unfortunate that he left."

This was the period in which Dunne was playing his best football for Ireland, as arguably the most important player in

He'd say something like that. And then he'd come up to you and say 'You know I didn't mean anything by that.' I'm like - 'You wouldn't even have said anything to me unless it had become public knowledge what you'd said, and people said 'hang on, that's a bit out of order'. He had no personal skills, you know what I mean? No understanding of who he was working with, the history of the club, how things had been before he came along, how difficult it was in the place. He was... just an idiot."

He went to Aston Villa, who were then managed by Martin O'Neill. "My debut was against Birmingham. Me and James Collins had both signed, gone straightaway on international duty. Came back on the Thursday, trained, trained on the Friday. So we ask him, what's the craic with free kicks, corners and all that? He

the Trapattoni-era team. I say to Dunne that I once heard an Irish player say of Trapattoni: "He says nothing to us before the game. He says nothing to us during the game. And he says nothing to us after the game."

"Yeah. But he said a lot in training. You know how he always goes on about the details, the details. So years ago they had lost a final at Juventus by a throw in, or something. So we kept constantly practicing this thing - how to defend against it. A throw in. We'd spend 15 minutes on someone throwing the ball in and the right-

> "SO WE ASK HIM, WHAT'S THE CRAIC WITH FREE KICKS, CORNERS AND ALL THAT? HE LOOKS AT US AND HE SAYS: 'THE SIZE OF THE TWO OF YOUSE. JUST GO AND FUCKING HEAD THE BALL.' THERE WAS NONE OF THIS, 'I WANT YOU IN THIS POSITION, YOU IN THAT POSITION' - IT WAS 'JUST GO AND HEAD THE BALL. THAT'S WHY I SIGNED YOUSE TWO."

winger and right-back working as a team to block it off. You think it's pointless - practicing throw-ins? The fuck are we practicing throw-ins for? But we were dead effective from them. We were very hard to break down. You knew where you had to be and what you had to do."

"So on Monday, we'd do the throw-in. On Tuesday, the block - I would pass the ball past a guy to the - supposedly - centre-forward. He'd have a defender behind him. And then I wasn't allowed to get the ball back, they had to block me. So they had to work as a team, it was all about working together, the full-back, the winger, the midfielder and centre-half."

"He'd lose his head over corners. Nine times out of ten we'd cleared the ball. But someone has been standing in the wrong place. Or the ball has gone over someone's head. And it's like - 'I can't fucking jump ten foot in the air - what can I do?' He'd say 'You don't know, you don't know!' I'd say 'I know what you're talking about, I understand you.' And he'd just go off on one. It was funny, in a way. You'd just watch him - 'Yeah, I understand what you're saying. I do get it - relax now. I understand where I have to be.' To us, professional footballers who'd played loads of games, it was like... schoolboy stuff. But I don't think we conceded a goal from a corner until we got to the Euros. And then Italy scored one against us, actually Spain scored one against us... OK, we'd fallen apart by that stage..."

"But that's when he did his work, in training. You'd think, I can't believe we're doing this again. I can't believe we're doing this again. Ten or fifteen minutes of the most boring training you've ever done in your life. You'd think that you'd instantly forget it. But you do it that regularly that when the match comes, you don't even have to think about it. Everyone knows where they are, everyone

knows what position they're supposed to be in. Which is why repetitive training is effective, you keep doing the same thing over and over, it has to sink in subconsciously, you just get better at it."

Never quite good enough for Trap. During a punditry gig on Italian TV last year, he claimed: "My Ireland team went out of the Euros qualifiers due to a mistaken throw-in at the 92nd minute." It was actually a a screwed-up free-kick in the corner against Austria, and it was in the World Cup qualifiers, not the Euros, but never mind.

***

I wonder how Dunne can disconnect so completely from football at the age of 37. It's been his whole life. What else is he going to do?

"That's it though. From the age of seven, the main thing was playing football all day. And it turned out to be my job. So I've been doing the same thing for thirty years, day in and day out. And now I've stopped. And you think... well; what am I gonna do? The answer is just... do whatever you want. It's just natural, whatever comes up."

Offers came to do TV punditry and at first he was reluctant.

"I kind of had a big hangup about it. All these ex-footballers, they must know how difficult it is to go out there and play. And then they go on TV and they slag everyone off. Fucking hell, have you not been in that situation where you've had a nightmare or you've made a mistake? You've done the last thing you wanted to do, you never want to make that mistake. And they just go and hammer everyone, I thought, I don't want to do that."

But he drifted into it anyway. First, he accepted an invitation to do some punditry on Premier

> "SO I'VE BEEN DOING THE SAME THING FOR THIRTY YEARS, DAY IN AND DAY OUT. AND NOW I'VE STOPPED. AND YOU THINK... WELL, WHAT AM I GONNA DO? THE ANSWER IS JUST... DO WHATEVER YOU WANT. IT'S JUST NATURAL, WHATEVER COMES UP."

League TV because it wouldn't be broadcast in England and Ireland. "I didn't want to be, you know, back in people's faces straightaway…" That turned out to be kind of fun, so he did some Champions League matches on TV3. Then he appeared on ITV to do the Ireland matches in the Euros. He liked travelling back to Ireland and England, meeting up with some old friends, feeling briefly as though he was part of the game again.

One unforeseen difficulty arose when he covered a couple of terrible Man City matches in the Champions League.

"It was City against Paris, then City

against Real Madrid in the semi-final first leg, which was shocking. Two shite matches - what do you say when the match is terrible? People are saying analyse it, tell us. I'm saying... 'they didn't play well.'"

I suggest that one useful strategy is to pick a victim…

"And then just hammer them? Yeah, that works. I watched RTE2 the other day after the Serbia match. I was laughing. Dunphy and Brady arguing, and I can see Didi just on the side, I can imagine what he'd be thinking in that situation... But it was good. OK, I think Dunphy was out of order in what he was saying about Glenn Whelan, hammering him. I mean he was hammering James McCarthy saying he should be out of the team, then he was saying Robbie Brady needs to be in midfield, and now he needs to go back to left-back... but it was interesting listening to them arguing, both really believing what they're saying. They can't both be right…"

"After I came home from the Euros, I said to my wife, "I really enjoyed that, doing the Euros, it was good fun. They were dead nice, all the people. But... I don't think I'll bother any more."

I don't get it. If you enjoyed it, why not do more of it?

"Well what happened was, I forgot about it, went back to England for a holiday in August. And then the day I got home, I got a call from BT. I didn't know anyone from BT, but they called me out of the blue, and said "sorry for contacting you like this, but would you like to do the Man City matches?" I thought, fucking hell, I'm here. I might as well do it."

I wonder if he has heard from the FAI about coming back to work in Irish football. It turns out the only contact he has with them these days is when he calls up looking to get tickets for his Dad to go to the Ireland matches.

Former internationals like Damien Duff, Keith Andrews, Kenny Cunningham, Mark Kinsella and his old Home Farm team-mate Stephen McPhail are now involved in FAI coaching roles. Dunne doesn't expect to be joining them.

"This is what annoys me about coaching badges. It's like, I can't coach because I don't have coaching badges. And it's like, surely I can coach a 15 year old how to defend? I don't need a coaching badge after playing 80 caps, or playing in England for 20 years. I know enough about it. At higher levels people want badges and stuff, but for kids… it's just another money-making scheme for people. It's just jobs for people. You're getting assessed by somebody who's never played a match at the highest level. And they're telling you what to do. I don't know what they can teach you. Unless it's like, I dunno, public speaking or, how to run a group… People who've never done anything in the game but they do their badges; so it's fine for them coach a team, but I can't? It's just stupid. I don't mean it in a bad way, but surely to God if you've

got so many experiences it should count for something."

I've heard other players complain privately that they didn't learn a lot on the coaching courses. But this is how the game works now: if you want to do the job, you need the badges. Is Dunne really saying that he hasn't done them because he doesn't think he'd learn anything?

"No. I just can't be arsed. I've no interest in being a coach, to be honest. The work itself would be good, I think… but it's too much. It's too much effort and time. The way it is, my kids are at a great age

> **"THE WAY IT IS, MY KIDS ARE AT A GREAT AGE WHEN I'M GETTING TO SPEND LOADS OF TIME WITH THEM. IT'S BRILLIANT. I'VE STOPPED DOING FOOTBALL, STOPPED BEING AWAY, STOPPED PREPARING OR RECOVERING ALL THE TIME. AND NOW IT'S JUST... FREEDOM.**

when I'm getting to spend loads of time with them. It's brilliant. I've stopped doing football, stopped being away, stopped preparing or recovering all the time. And now it's just… freedom.

"Right now, I'm free. I can literally do anything. I'm going to the Caribbean in November for a month. I've never had a holiday at that time of year. We'll take the kids out of school for it, because, for me, to give them different experiences as they grow up, that's the main thing. So if I was to say to them now, I'm gonna go back and be a coach…"

So instead, he's taking it easy. Playing a bit of five a side. Going down to Italy on the boat. People who work all the time are always saying they'd love to spend more time with their family. So that's what Dunne is doing.

Maybe he'll be back in football one day. But it doesn't sound like he'll waste too much time planning ahead. After 20 years of the professional grind, it's time to take each day as it comes.

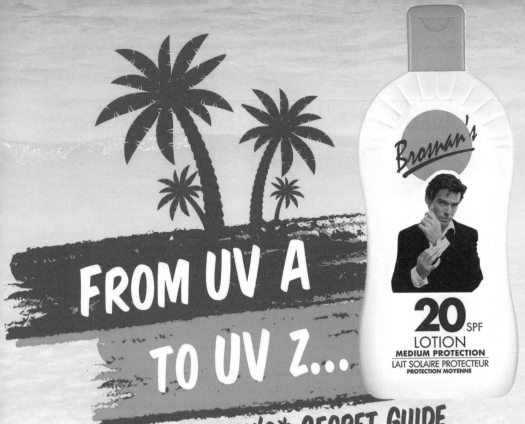

FROM UV A TO UV Z...

PIERCE BROSNAN'S* SECRET GUIDE TO THE WORLDWIDE SPORTS TANNING SCENE

Simon made his name as one of Hollywood's go-to movie extras in the early 1980s (drunken frat boy at house party in *Can't Buy Me Love* and schoolyard bully in *Girls Just want to Have Fun*), before making a smooth and successful transition to the then-more-lucrative tanning consultancy business on the advice of his friend **, Hollywood legend and tan sensation Pierce Brosnan.

After working the American hotel chain circuit for a few years, Simon was headhunted by private clients such as Burt Reynolds and David Hasselhoff who at the time were shaping popular culture and the way people thought about sunbathing. The industry was booming; catching rays was no longer a leisure activity but a means to assert your dominance over the less-tanned. Riding the wave of an industry that couldn't fail, Simon was dubbed the King of Complexion by Rolling Stone magazine, and Time listed him as one of the 100 most influential people of the decade.

Sadly, the industry abruptly went bust in the 90s with the emergence of milky faced stars such as Kurt Cobain, Kate Moss and Brett Anderson, and so Simon was reluctantly forced into pursuing a career in sports broadcasting in Ireland. That fire never died, however, and in recent years the emergence of the likes of Snooki, Peter Andre and Ronaldo helped reignite an old passion. Throughout the decades, Pierce has never wavered and stayed true to his tan and himself.

* Words by Simon Hick and Pierce Brosnan

Tan Objective: Tawny
Chosen celeb: Rob Kearney

It's great to see one of your own excel on the world stage, giving hope to all Celts that they too can one day reach the top of the pigment pile. As the most tanned man in Louth, Rob knew from an early age that he could go places, but coming good on that talent isn't always straightforward with life sometimes throwing up unforeseen obstacles. Rob was unluckily sent to school in deepest Kildare which meant sun exposure was hard earned throughout his teenage years.

Once the pro contract came in from Leinster, however, Rob quickly made up for lost time by getting his skin tan-ready. Many people underestimate the importance of moisturising; not our Rob. Aloe Vera, Shea Butter, Serum - find out what works for you and lather it on three to four times a day. The other thing to note about Rob is his self-restraint. Its a gentleman's tan, he's not trying to overdo it. In the wrong hands, this skin tone could enter Jersey Shore territory, but Rob understands that with great power comes great responsibility, and always keeps it understated. For any young kids out there looking to become a full-time tanned person, check out Rob's technique. Textbook!

Tan Objective: The Greek Fisherman
Chosen celeb: Cristiano Ronaldo

Il capo dei capi of the tan game, the MVP of UVB, Ronaldo has it all; natural born gifts, an innate competitiveness, and a relentless work ethic. On a yacht, by the pool, at the team hotel, on the edge of the pitch at training - CR7 never misses an opportunity to worship his Solar God. There's just no way around it; if you want to achieve full Greek Fisherman status you're gonna have to put the hours in. It's a long hard road, one on which you will have to take real risks with your suncream factor. Start considering midday sun sessions, zero factor oil, holidays near the equator, and you may even want to consider a change of career. This one is not for you office dummies.

I don't use the phrase 'gamechanger' lightly, but what Ronaldo has done sets the tone, literally and metaphorically, for all future generations. He has achieved the Holy Grail of tans, which is to say that if he were to stop sunbathing today and never see another ray of light for the rest of his life, he would still be tanned on his deathbed. A heartwarming thought for us all to dwell on during these long northern European winters.

Tan Objective: Transatlantic Pilot
Chosen sports celeb: Aidan O'Shea

I love somebody that wants to make the best of themselves, in spite of their obvious genetic disadvantages, and let's be honest, we all feel a little sorry for Aidan and the DNA hand that he's been dealt. With the right focus, training and diet, however, Aidan has gone from being a mere Brian O'Driscoll (you have to wonder is Brian even trying?) to a Bradley Cooper, and could, one day, maybe even graduate to Ryan Reynolds levels of tan.

If that is to be considered a realistic goal, however, the first thing I'd say to Aidan is drop the football career. GAA success can be especially damaging to a young tanner as it demands a lot of gym work and indoor meetings in those key summer months when the UVA and UVB rays are at their strongest.

Another thing fans should note about Aidan is his consistency of tan through all seasons. The secret to a golden glow isn't just about the hot days in August, it's also about getting up early on a cold January morning and making your way to a spray salon or a sunbed outlet.

Tan Objective: Marbella Gold
Chosen sports celeb: Frank Lampard

Frank realised quite early in life that the more tanned you are, the happier you are, and set about making it as a footballer so that he could afford to holiday in sunny places. Frank seems to glow from the inside out, a mixture of a great personality and more likely, a constant supply of Beta Carotene supplements.

Frank's hero growing up was Brigitte Bardot as he instantly recognised one of the greats at work. This was a tan earned the hard way…. by the beaches, pools and outdoor cocktail bars of the French Riviera. It also set a template that lasts to this day: the all over body tan.

Frank, crucially, has an encyclopaedic knowledge of the ozone layer and where the biggest holes can be found. A word of caution for those with a similar skin tone to Frank, however - body hair is not an option here; Marbella Gold looks best on a completely bald torso, preferably accessorised with a pectoral tattoo or a subtle neck chain.

TANNED LEGENDS TO INSPIRE YOU THROUGHOUT THE SPORTING ERAS:

From left to right: Graeme Souness, Steve Beaton (early Steve Beaton obviously), John Maughan, Sue Barker, Maurice Fitzgerald (legs)

**Pierce Brosnan has not endorsed or contributed to this piece in any way or ever spoken to Simon. He has gone on the record as saying he admired Simon's performance in Can't Buy Me Love.

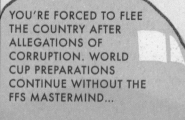

YOU'RE FORCED TO FLEE THE COUNTRY AFTER ALLEGATIONS OF CORRUPTION. WORLD CUP PREPARATIONS CONTINUE WITHOUT THE FFS MASTERMIND...

...BUT YOUR ABILITY TO GET THE JOB DONE GETS RECOGNISED IN POLITICAL CIRCLES

"WE'RE GONNA WIN SOOOOOO MUCH, YOU MAY GET TIRED OF WINNING"

YOU ARE INVITED TO THE OLYMPIC GAMES AS PART OF THE RUSSIAN FEDERATION, YOU TAKE THE OPPORTUNITY TO MAKE YOUR MARK ON THE WORLD STAGE.

"WHO IS THIS GUY?"

POLICE STORM A ROOM WHERE YOU ARE INJECTING A RUSSIAN ATHLETE. YOU'VE BEEN CAUGHT!

DO YOU

A. OWN UP TO THE AUTHORITIES, ACCEPT YOUR FATE AS A TOP-CLASS SPORTS ADMINISTRATOR IS OVER AND RETURN TO IRELAND?

GO TO PAGE 35

B. PLAN AN ESCAPE ROUTE?

GO TO PAGE 109

New York, We Love You

For three years, we'd been reading the #PBESO emails about trying to make friends in New York and the subway journey's into Manhattan with nothing but your Second Captains podcast buddies for company. So in April, we rolled into NYC for a packed out show. Thanks so much to everyone who came to the live rooftop recording and put up with the freezing cold. We'll be back in a slightly warmer time of the year in 2017.

From left to right: 'The Greyhound' Owen Roe Kavanagh, Ken, Andy Lee, Mark, Eoin, Des Bishop, John Duddy, Henry Shefflin, Murph and Sean Cunningham - the boss at Brass Monkey'

These trips don't happen without the kind help of our friends at Aer Lingus and the real plus-point of promotional photo-shoots is how uncomfortable Ken is.

Our live show was at the Brass Monkey bar in the Meat Packing District. After introducing Henry Shefflin to the crowd, we heard from Des Bishop & Grant Wahl, Andy Lee & John Duddy (which Sheff sneakily watched from the window). The night had it all, including some flashers from the nearby Standard Hotel and Des pouring pints for The King.

We packed a lot in to 5 days including an Andy Lee interview with world title challenger Patrick Hyland. Andy and Mark took in training at the Mendez gym and lunch with Hyland and his coach Paschal Collins. Ken met Roger Bennett of Men in Blazers in their Manhattan studio and Eoin and Murph travelled to Randall's Island to spend time with the great Johnny Glynn.

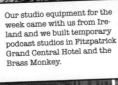

Our studio equipment for the week came with us from Ireland and we built temporary podcast studios in Fitzpatrick Grand Central Hotel and the Brass Monkey.

We also took in Trump protests, beers, Manhattan runs that nearly killed us, and most importantly, romantic central park shots.

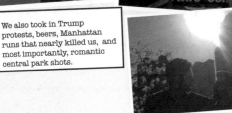

Congratulations!

YOU DID THE RIGHT THING! YOU GO ON TO HAVE A LONG AND SUCCESSFUL CAREER AS THE GREATEST SPORTS ADMINISTRATOR THE WORLD HAS EVER SEEN! ALL OF THIS WILL BE YOURS! YOU HAVE **EARNED:**

THE LOVE OF YOUR FANS

A CELEBRITY LIFESTYLE

A MOVIE CAREER

THE RESPECT OF THE MEDIA

THE SKILLS TO BE A RACONTEUR PAR EXCELLANCE!

RICHES BEYOND YOUR WILDEST DREAMS!

THE FREEDOM TO NOT HAVE TO WEAR SHOES!

SECOND CAPTAINS
GAME ZONE

" WHAT? WHAT ARE YOU LOOKING AT? YES, I'M FUCKING WEARING WHITE SOCKS WITH MY BLACK DRESS SHOES, BIG FUCKING DEAL. I'VE BEEN FORCED TO INTRODUCE THE NEXT SECTION OF THE ANNUAL SO HERE'S THE BULLSHIT QUIZ SECTION INGENIOUSLY ENTITLED 'GAME ZONE'. IF YOU ENJOY THE FOLLOWING PAGES, YOU NEED TO GROW UP."

DON'T WORRY, THE FUN ISN'T OVER YET. MEASURE THE SIZE OF YOUR SPORTS BRAIN IN THE FINAL AND GREATEST SECTION OF OUR BOOK. HERE'S STEPHEN THE SECOND CAPTAINS STINK BADGER WITH THE DETAILS!
(WE TOLD YOU HE WAS A PRICK)

CONTINUED OVER PAGE

THE SUPER SEXY
SCOTTY TOO HOTTY EVANS QUIZ

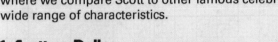

We all followed the fortunes of Badminton bad boy Scott Evans in Rio as he sizzled his way through the men's draw, thrilling fans with his mastery of the shuttlecock, and his demented celebrations.

We feel the best way to honour his Olympic achievements is of course with a Scotty too hotty Second Captains quiz, where we compare Scott to other famous celebrities on a wide range of characteristics.

1. Scott or Dallas
Scott's topless celebrations went viral during the Olympics, becoming known worldwide as the Full Evans. Can you tell us if the following quotes are from Scott himself, or another well known striptease artist, Dallas from Magic Mike.

A: 'The law says you cannot touch.....but I think I see a lotta lawbreakers up in this house tonight'

B: "If I win tomorrow, there might be a bit more than my t-shirt coming off!"

2. Scott can walk the walk, but he can talk the talk too. Tell us if the following quotes are from Scott 'lord of the strings' Evans, or renowned heavyweight hard man 'iron' Mike Tyson.

A: "I just have this thing inside me that wants to eat and conquer. Maybe it's egotistical, but I have it in me. I don't want to be a tycoon. I just want to conquer people and their souls.

B: "I got quite a surprise that the shuttles were even slower than what we have been training with for the last five or six days.

HEADLESS TORSO...

Anyone can get their top off, but not everyone has the physique to back it up. Ireland's best ever badminton player has more than earned the right to put his goods on show. As Scott says, if the bar ain't bendin', you're just pretendin'. Below are pictures of sporting celebs, minus their head. Can you tell which one is Scott?

(A)   **(B)**   **(C)**

Answers on Page 108

FINAL SCORE:
3 - CONGRATULATIONS, YOU TRULY ARE BADMINTON TO THE BONE!
2 - YOU HAVE GOOD BADMINTON KNOWLEDGE BUT YOU WOULD BE OUT OF YOUR DEPTH IF IN CONVERSATION WITH SCOTT AT AN AFTER MATCH FUNCTION. MUST TRY HARDER.
1 - STOP WASTING OUR TIME. GO TAKE UP A WIMP SPORT LIKE TENNIS.
0 - SCOTT IS PERSONALLY INSULTED THAT YOU EVEN BROWSED THIS SECTION OF THE ANNUAL.

ROGER BLACK'S SPORTS QUOTATIONS OF 2016

From Leicester City's Premier League odyssey, to Ireland's Euro romp, to the politics and parties of Rio; 2016 was a non-stop sports riot. Below are some of the best quotes from 2016, but can you name the source? *Not actually compiled by Roger Black but hopefully his never say die attitude will inspire you

1. "And then the guy pulled out his gun, he cocked it, put it to my forehead and he said: 'Get down', and I put my hands up, I was like 'whatever!'

2. "It's clear bullying, In Slovenia, we would have indicted Mourinho and asked for the highest penalty - three years in prison." What crime was Slovenia FifPro member Dejan Stefanovic referring to?

3. "Every time you get a knock, you don't have to go for a scan or take pain killers or have two days recovery or sit in the pool for an hour and a half. It's a man's game we're playing, believe it or not."

4. "Its been the perfect response. Start again. Keep dominating. Keep getting pressure on the Iceland back four. The only thing they have got is the big boy up front, Sigthórsson, who really...... sssssss........OH MY WORD....ooooohhhh..."

5. "Robbie Brady you absolute ride."

6. 'An excellent meeting'

7. "About 80% of you here have at some point scratched your balls. Therefore, everything is good."

8. "Over the past two years, my work ethic has increased from 10 per cent to 80 per cent. I have really started working hard over the past two years."

Answers on Page 108

MOSES HIGHTOWER FROM POLICE ACADEMY'S SPORTS MOVIE QUOTES

Fancy yourself as a sports movie buff? Reckon you know your Bull Durhams from your Tin Cups? Well prove it by working out which famous sports movie gave rise to each of the following memorable quotes. Bonus point for the name of the character or actor who uttered the quote.

1. "You see Billy it's like this, you either smoke or you get smoked.
And you got smoked."

2. "I must break you."

3. "You don't understand. I coulda had class. I coulda been a contender. I coulda been somebody, instead of a bum, which is what I am."

4. "I'm going to take a hot bath, I'm getting cold just thinking about all this ice."

5. "I'm the best you ever seen, Fats. I'm the best there is. Now even if you beat me, I'm still the best."

7. "It's a very personal, very important thing. Hell, it's a family motto."

8. "Try and make it a clean break, will ya?"

9. (Whispered): "This crowd has gone deadly silent. Cinderella story. Out of nowhere. A former greenskeeper now about to become the Masters champion..."

10. "Hate put me in prison. Love's gonna bust me out."

11. "A grain of rice is going to tip the scale. Just remember that lads, a grain of rice will tip the scale."

THE ULTIMATE OLYMPIAN – IDENTIFY THE BODY PARTS

We have taken the best bits of numerous competitors from Rio 2016 and welded them together in order to engineer an Olympian so perfect that he/she/it would only need to consume the bare minimum of performance-enhancing drugs in order to guarantee a medal. We need you to identify the owner of each body part.

Answers on Page 108

104

-THE BEAUTIFUL GAME-

The football manager look has come a long way in the last decade. There was a time when broken blood vessels, open pores and a Scottish accent were all you needed to make it in the beautiful game. With the influx of foreign managers to the Premier League, however, the sidelines have become a catwalk. Nothing but a tight butt and a tailored suit will do and with that, we have seen the emergence of the managerial makeover. From Conte's hair to Brendan's teeth to Phil's tan; in 2016, DNA no longer holds you back. For any budding managers out there, we have put together a style guide to help you make it to the next level.

Conte's hair - thick and lustrous, reliable in humid conditions and on windy days. An Italian masterpiece.

Brendan Rodgers' teeth - made their first appearance in 2013, still adjusting to their new home (Brendan's mouth) but certainly a template there for young managers. Go big, go white, and always have them on show.

Steve McLaren's brolly - why do football managers stand in the rain? You'll catch your death. Steve transformed his image with the bold move to stand under a brolly when managing England. His career has since gone from strength to strength.

Pep's Pants - His teams don't quit, and neither does his butt. That's why he gets those suits painted on. Yes they rip at the crotch from time time, but its worth it for the two eggs in a hanky look.

Phil Brown's fake tan - The life of a football manager is not conducive to good skin, so why not cover the imperfections with a chocolatey brown fake tan? Smart move Phil.

Herve Renard's body - Herve has made a name for himself in African football, but the first thing on his CV is his deltoid definition. That's why he gets those white cotton shirts tailored super tight, and if he wins a cup you best believe everything is coming off.

Jose's cuban heels - Jose is not a tall man but he more than makes up for this with his generous heel lifts, a modern version of the Cuban Heel. There has never been a short POTUS, and the same applies to football managers. That's right, Sammy Lee.

SECOND CAPTAINS
STRESS-REDUCTION CORNER

Colour in our cover and win prizes...
and therapy for that old brain of yours

Everyone knows Colouring-in is the new Kale and here's a healthy feast straight out of the Second Captains kitchen. Drop that bloody iPhone, get your markers out, take some precious time to yourself and add your own personal touch to Dan Leydon's delightful front cover. Ah doesn't that feel good?

Now add your name, pick up that precious iPhone , take a photo of your masterpiece and tweet it to us @SecondCaptains. Our favourite 5 will win Second Captains merchandise APLENTY. We hope you enjoy this sacred 20 minutes of zen.

Name: _____

Age: _____

Sketch Box

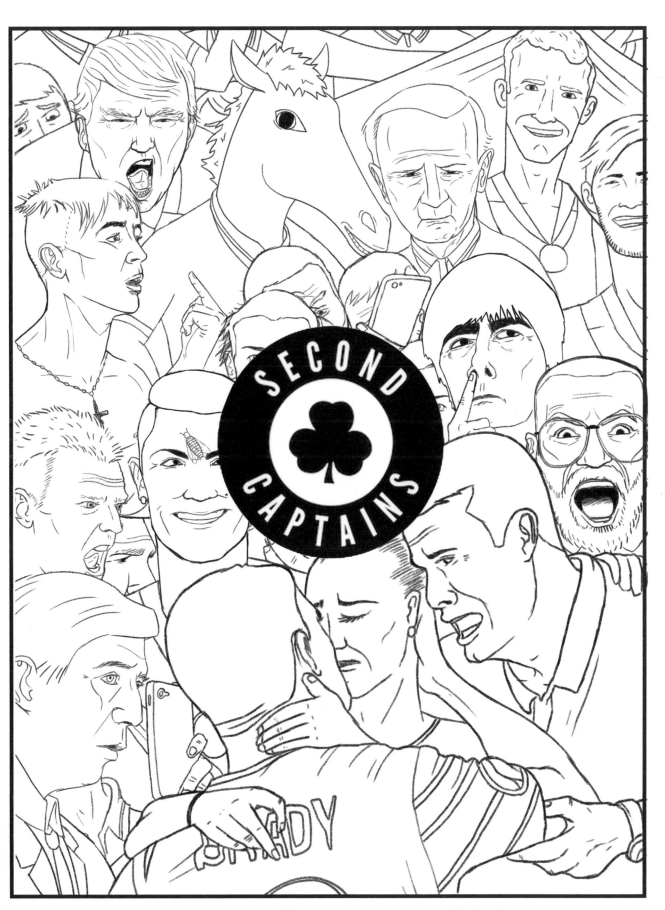

SPORTS ANNUAL VOL.2

SECOND CAPTAINS
GAME ZONE
— ANSWERS PAGE —

THE SUPER SEXY SCOTTY TOO HOTTY EVANS QUIZ:

1. Scott or Dallas
(A) Ans - Dallas
(B) Ans - Scott Evans

2. Scott or Mike
(A) Ans - Mike Tyson
(B) Ans - Scott Evans

3. Headless torso
(A): Ronaldo
(B): Scott
(C): McGregor

ROGER BLACK'S SPORTS QUOTATIONS OF 2016

1. Ans - Ryan Lochte

2. Ans - Jose Mourinho asking Bastian Schweinsteiger to train alone with Manchester United's under 23's

3. Ans - Roy Keane on the eve of Euro 2016

4. Ans - Steve McLaren on Sky Sports

5. Ans - Shane Lowry

6. Ans - Pat Hickey on his meeting with Shane Ross

7. Ans - Lukas Podolski on Jogi Loew's sideline hand trouser rummaging, hand sniffing antics

8. Ans - Mario Balotelli

THE ULTIMATE OLYMPIAN - IDENTIFY THE BODY PARTS

- Simone Biles legs
- Usain Bolt's torso
- Michael Phelps' arms in wingspan mode
- Ryan Lochte's neck
- Mo Farah's face
- Neymar's 100% Jesus headband

MOSES HIGHTOWER FROM POLICE ACADEMY'S SPORTS MOVIE QUOTES

1. Movie: White Men Can't Jump
  Bonus point: Sidney Deane (played by Wesley Snipes)

2. Movie: Rocky IV
  Bonus point: Ivan Drago (played by Dolph Lundgren)

3. Movie: On The Waterfront
  Bonus point: Terry Malloy (played by Marlon Brando)
  Also acceptable: Raging Bull
  Bonus point: Jake LaMotta (played by Robert De Niro)

4. Movie: Cool Runnings
  Bonus point: Sanka Coffie (played by Doug E. Doug)

5. Movie: The Hustler
  Bonus point: "Fast" Eddie Felson (played by Paul Newman)

6. Movie: Jerry Maguire
  Bonus point: Rod Tidwell (played by Cuba Gooding Jr.)

7. Movie: Escape to Victory
  Bonus point: Tony Lewis (Allied goalkeeper. Played by Kevin O'Callaghan)

8. Movie: Caddyshack
  Bonus point: Carl Spackler (played by Bill Murray)

9. Movie: The Hurricane
  Bonus point: Rubin "Hurricane" Carter (played by Denzel Washington)

10. Movie: Marooned
  Bonus point: Páidí Ó Sé (played by Páidí Ó Sé)

We want to end the annual with a sincere thank you to YOU, the person reading this book right now (unless you are just borrowing a copy from someone). Obviously the biggest thanks of all go to the people who bought last year's book as well as this year's. Thanks too to everyone who just bought last year's book - but then again if you're in that bracket and you're reading this, it means you're just borrowing this one which sort of diminishes the thanks deserved. In fact, if you are part of this group we rescind that thanks. This is getting complicated, here's a breakdown of our thank you levels.

People who bought 2 books – extremely thankful
People who bought this year's book – very thankful
People who bought last year's book but not this years book – thankful but hurt
People who got the book for free - meh
Relations who got the book for free - not thankful
People who borrowed the book both years - fuck you

Thanks to Ciaran Walsh and Trevor Finnegan, our brilliant production and design team from Sweatshop and Revert Design who have done some gorgeous work with us on the book again this year – you have come into our office, worked diligently alongside us, and not stolen anything, and if that's not the dictionary definition of a successful partnership, then we don't know what is.

Huge thanks to our friend Billy Stickland and everyone at Inpho for their help in making the book happen.

We loved working with our talented and super-sound contributors, Amy O'Connor and Anton Ingi Sveinbjörnsson., and with our amazing illustrator CIEMAY (Colm McAthlaoich), and a special thank you to Oisin McConville and Richie Sadlier for devoting so much of their precious time to ridiculous photo-shoots. Thanks too to to Dan Leydon for his brilliant work on the cover.

The biggest thanks of all to everyone who listens to the podcasts and radio show or tunes into the TV show. Thank you for getting in touch with us online and for being so kind and supportive to us over the years (even if you just borrowed the annuals).

Finally, a Thomas Bach/Pat Hickey-sized hug to our families, partners, sons, daughters and friends

First published in 2016 by Second Captains Limited

secondcaptains.com
editor@secondcaptains.com

ISBN: 978-0-9934291-1-8

Produced by: Second Captains and Sweatshop Media
Designed by: Revert Design
Illustrations by CIEMAY, Dan Leydon, Trevor Finnegan
Photography throughout with thanks to Billy Strickland and Inpho Photography
Edited by Mark Horgan

Writing from: Ken Early, Simon Hick, Mark Horgan, Eoin McDevitt,
Ciaran Murphy, Amy O'Connor and Anton Ingi Sveinbjörnsson.